The Hopes of Snakes

The Hopes of Snakes

and Other Tales from the Urban Landscape

LISA COUTURIER

BEACON
150

Beacon Press
Boston

Beacon Press
25 Beacon Street
Boston, Massachusetts 02108-2892
www.beacon.org

Beacon Press books are published under the auspices of
the Unitarian Universalist Association of Congregations.

08 07 06 05 8 7 6 5 4 3 2

This book is printed on acid-free paper that meets the uncoated paper
ANSI/NISO specifications for permanence as revised in 1992.

Text design by Patricia Duque Campos
Composition by Wilsted & Taylor Publishing Services

Library of Congress Cataloging-in-Publication Data
Couturier, Lisa.
  The hopes of snakes : and other tales from the urban landscape /
Lisa Couturier.
    p. cm.
  ISBN 0-8070-8564-2 (cloth : alk. paper)
  1. Urban animals—New York (State)—New York—Anecdotes.
  2. Urban animals—Washington Metropolitan Area—Anecdotes.
  I. Title.

QL195.C68 2004
591.75'6—dc22   2004015081

The author gratefully acknowledges permission to reprint "Rediscovering the Potomac"
from *Heart of a Nation: Writers and Photographers Inspired by the American Landscape* (National
Geographic Society, 2000).

Several essays in this book appeared in different forms in the following journals and
anthologies: "Reversing the Tides" appeared in *The River Reader* (Lyons Press, 1998). "Off
Being God" is an expanded version of "Spiritual Gypsy," published in *Iris,* Fall/Winter
1997. "Heirloom" appeared in *Potomac Review,* Fall 2000. "For All the Girls Who Couldn't
Walk into the Woods" was published as "Walking in the Woods" in *Iris,* Winter/Spring
1996. "A Banishment of Crows" appeared in *American Nature Writing, 2000: A Celebration
of Women Writers* (Oregon State University Press, 2000). "The Hopes of Snakes" appeared in
The Gallatin Review, 2003. "Take the Long Way Home" was published as "A Clandestine
Freedom" in *The Mountain Reader* (Lyons Press, 2000).

For Kirk,
for our girls, Madeleine and Lucienne,
and for the animals

Be careful not to say

Anything too final. Whatever
Is unsure is possible, and life is bigger
Than flesh. Beyond reach of thought
Let imagination figure

Your hope.

"Testament" by Wendell Berry

Introduction

You are in borderless touch with the closest things,
and, what is more, distance is not sufficient
to separate you from things far away.
Kahlil Gibran

I knew the truth at twenty-three that my life, or at least a good part
of it, was meant to be lived someplace other than the suburbs of
Washington, D.C., where, like most Americans raised on the East
Coast, I had grown up as a bona fide suburban child chasing grass-
hoppers across carpets of green grass and dashing through sprin-
klers of summer. If my leaving Washington in the mid-eighties had
been a case of disliking the area, I would not have returned to live
here, as I did in 1998, returned to everything suburban that I knew
before: the fiery autumn of the Potomac River charging below the
ridge on which is built my family's old stone cottage, the green
snakes in the fig tree, the crows and hawks that have called me back
into the woodsy underbrush of my past. But isn't it the case that,
wherever we spend our childhoods, we dream, sometimes, of the
mighty trees not native to our childhood landscape, trees we cannot
begin to climb unless we set out for a new forest?

As it happened, Manhattan became my new forest in 1985, a
place to canter through the unpredictability of a life, which is perhaps some of what was missing from the landscape of a suburban
childhood, where I had galloped a million times in the same saddle
of perfect lawns. New York on the other hand, as I soon learned,
bucks a person over and over. Just when you're comfortably moseying along, New York will throw you. Want to be kicked out of

what you believed you were? Want to be lassoed? New York will do these things for you. It is alive in this way. Present. Attendant. It dares you to trot into its canyons of dark and unknown streets, to cross its paths of opposition, to drink from its fountains of divergence. Every morning you stroll into the city's leafy offerings and are willing, in the rain, to allow your heart to be bitten, bucked, or thrown down because you understand that in doing so New York is better able to show you what you were sent there to see, which, though part of you now, ultimately are not the things of architecture or theater, fashion, opera, or the Village, but instead, simply and importantly, your self, bareback.

For someone like me who has desired little except a closeness to animals, and who craved this so strongly that without them I often felt fractured and lost, then the creatures of New York City, once discovered, became healers in a way. They defined for me what was sacred in the city and what might be sacred in a life. A glossy ibis gliding into the lake in Central Park? Peregrine falcons hunting over the East River? Black racers and box turtles moving across Brooklyn? This is disequilibrium. The sense of getting bucked. This is the city or, rather, the heart of the city—the landscape— saying, *look here . . . you are imbued with these lives as with any theater or architecture.* Within the confines of the city and its suburbs were animals as deserving of reverence and respect as any inhabiting wilder terrains. Here were animals living amidst the untold millions of human demands made on the landscape each day, animals living largely unnoticed, flying, swimming, slithering, and crawling through territories that, though stolen from them now, once were theirs.

Though of course there are differences, it is also the case that the New York and Washington metro areas, both part of the Northeastern megalopolis, support similar life forms. Washington delineates the lower part of the Northeastern corridor and New York the middle, while the upper reach would be Boston, birthplace of my parents and home to members of my extended Irish-American family, a few of whom appear in these stories here and there. The suburbs of Washington and the city of New York have been the landscapes of my life. I have known no other places as well. And this is perhaps what New York taught me best: that I was and always would be inextricably bound to portions of the most densely humanized landscape in America and to its creatures living among us: heron and egret, Canada goose, coyote, peregrine falcon and red-tailed hawk, black rat snake, vulture, crow.

With every year that passed while I was in Manhattan, I began to realize I might never have been captured by the city and its creatures were it not for the suburban and urban landscape of the Potomac River watershed that had raised me, that had seeped into my cells like a cicada that burrows into the earth and emerges much later, at a twilight in its life, to climb up through the underbrush and into the branches of its childhood—the place from which it had fallen nearly seventeen years before. And now, in Washington, I realize that New York City is with me still, that it never left the way I thought it might. When every night about half past eight, the Canada geese fly from the Potomac over my cottage to the field of rich grass surrounding D.C.'s Dalecarlia Reservoir, I instantly remember the geese threading their way over the Upper East Side toward Central Park's reservoir. The red-tailed hawks in D.C. feather through me as ardently as those that hunted behind New York's Metropolitan Museum of Art. And at times, when I am asked where I live, I scribble *412 Ridge,* which is a combination of my two addresses, part New York, part Washington, both all tangled up with hawks and coyotes, crows and snakes, and the peach and pink skies dripping into the Potomac and the East River.

In the end, this collection of tales idles in that interior space where life is lived, viscerally, in more than one place at the same time. Each of us is a collection in the making, a collection of our landscapes, of our dreams, of the people in our lives. And though the canopy of one's life—both metaphorical and literal—might truly physically spread over large terrains of the earth, the treetops, the human and the nonhuman, the backyards and fields blossom, emotionally, all in one body. A body that feels the world enter: through memory and patterns of experience; through those we come to know and love as well as those we've loved so long; through the sensuality of the land and the stories of its inhabitants. Out there is a world ready to ride through us, to hoof its way straight to the veins or to meander over the muscles, like the slow passing of dark thunder clouds.

Though the stories in *The Hopes of Snakes* are arranged chronologically for the most part—with those written earlier and primarily based in the New York metro area composing the first part of the book and those written later and primarily based in Washington finishing up—a fair number of them weave nearly equally between both places; and thus it is not necessary to read a certain one before another. A curiosity about coyotes and women, or a longing for rivers and egrets? It will not matter, really, which is read first.

I believe that snakes have hopes, as do we all; and it is my hope that these stories about the urban landscape, about its people and creatures, speak, if to nothing else, to your heart.

Reversing the Tides

There was a child went forth every day,
And the first object he looked upon and received with
wonder or pity or love or dread, that object he became, ...
The horizon's edge, the flying seacrow, the fragrance
of saltmarsh
and shoremud...
Walt Whitman

The story is told in my family that when I was a year old my parents took me to the beach at Sandy Hook, New Jersey, which from the shoreline has a view of Manhattan. They took me out to the edge, where the sand meets the rocks, marking the intersection of Sandy Hook Bay, Lower New York Bay, and the Atlantic Ocean. My father lifted me up on his shoulders and my parents pointed to New York City. They say I looked. They say I saw the city then, on a clear day.

For many years I lived in Manhattan, and every day I walked to the East River—which, although big and wide as most people might imagine a river to be, is technically a tidal strait and part of the larger Hudson estuary ecosystem that surrounds Manhattan.

On my walks to the river, the wind, carrying the water's salt scent, surrounded me; and I was pulled to its estuarine currents. To get near the river's side I walked along a tar path that began at the end of my street and wound through a manicured park, around the mayor's mansion, and over a small grassy hill. Coming to the top of the hill, I always anticipated what the water would be like at my favorite spot on the river—Hell Gate, named so for the tangling of

I

tides that mix here: the Atlantic tide travels up the Manhattan arm of the East River to collide with the tide of the Long Island Sound and the current of the Harlem River. Some days the tides looked as though they were fighting. Dark olive green waters hit and chopped at each other and swirled and spiraled all at once. Other times nothing, every drop of water seemed to be just strolling along, friendly—as if water could sigh. I cleared the hill, walked under an American basswood tree growing in a triangle of grass, and stopped to let the wind blow over me. I took the air into my body, consciously swallowed it, gave my lungs—my entire being—a fix of the river's essence.

The smell of the water was as close as I could get to the river itself. There was no access, no great green shoreline. Looking at the river was more like looking at a mangy pound dog when you really wanted to see a shiny-furred, well-muscled purebred, its tail wagging. This body of water, like most of the waters around New York City, is for the most part surrounded by the dirty environment of the human world—fuel tanks, abandoned buildings, highways, skyscrapers, and such. But recently a bit of nature's more wild presence has returned to the river: butterflies, seaweed swaying over rocks, seagulls laughing, Canada geese flying in their autumn V, striped bass passing through from the Long Island Sound to the Hudson River, snapping turtles who've survived, somehow and somewhere, over the last four centuries in New York waters, American eels who swim to the Sargasso Sea to lay their eggs and whose young make the thousand-mile return trip to the city, peregrine falcons who nest twenty blocks downriver but hunt and fly up near where I lived, cormorants, herons, and egrets.

When I was by the river, which itself was so stripped—of its wetlands, of its shoreline, of its purity through pollution and abuse —I shed my own urban skin, a general impatience with things slow-moving, to listen to the movement of the river and to its waves against the rocks. The rippling of the water soothed me, as though its sound fused with my blood to calm me. Often, when the sun reflected pink and orange on the river in early evening, flocks of starlings or sparrows exploded out from the park's trees and circled out over the water as though they were riding an airborne roller coaster. They flew back over me, their wings beating against their bodies, and returned to the park. As the sky darkened, the birds settled in for the night and I began my walk home, envious that the birds, unlike me, were safe in the park at night by the river. If it was a summer evening, I left the river's side during a concert of cricket song with a light show of fireflies.

It's been a while since I stopped being surprised by nature in New York City, which is, after all, simply a name we've given this landscape—a label meaningless to the birds, the turtles, the river. Besides, writes James Hillman, the Jungian psychologist, the "Greek word for city, *polis*, ... draws from a pool of meanings related to water... *polis* locates city in the wet regions of the soul.... We need but remember that the city, the *metro-polis* means at root a streaming, flowing, thronging Mother. We are her children, and she can nourish our imaginations if we nourish hers."

Walking the river's promenade and looking across at Roosevelt Island, I think of a local legend, Thomas Maxey. He knew something about the wet regions of his soul, from whence his feelings and dreams informed his life and helped him nourish the riverscape. It is said he was a bit of a madman who was quite fond of birds. Shortly after the Civil War, Maxey built a fort at the tip of Roosevelt Island, just below Hell Gate; and in front of the fort, he erected a gate that was somehow designed to be used as a nesting site for wild geese. On the gate he wrote this message: I INVITE THE FOWLS AND THE BIRDS OF THE AIR TO ENTER.

Could it be that Maxey wasn't mad, just in love with the birds and the river? Perhaps he simply sensed what writer Thomas Moore says now: "Maybe one function of love is to cure us of an anemic imagination, a life emptied of romantic attachment and abandoned to reason."

Of course there must be biological reasons why the animals have returned to the East River—a body of water that, according to some accounts, was so toxic it would burn a ship's hull clean if the ship was docked in the river for a few days. Even as recently as the 1950s, sewage and pollutants from manufacturing plants were poured into the river. And it wasn't until the Clean Water Act of 1972 that New York finally stopped thinking of the river as its toilet. Until then people were dumping raw sewage into it daily. (Even now, when it rains more than an inch and a half, sewage treatment plants along the river overflow into it.) And today, although there are still PCBs and other toxins in the river's sediments, the East River is staging a comeback, which, according to local news reports, has environmental officials somewhat mystified. Nevertheless, oxygen levels are up; coliform bacteria (indicating the level of sewage) is down; amphipods—food for fish—are back, as are the crabs and minnows herons feed on; apparently, biodiversity is on the rise.

The river is making enormous changes, as is the city. The New York City Department of Environmental Protection reportedly has invested over a billion dollars to research the contamination of the East River and other parts of the estuary.

Environmental science: What is it but a way to rationalize our longings for interdependence and interrelationship?

Environmental legislation: What is it if not a desire for deep change, a kind of compassion for the earth?

For years I thought of the East River as nothing more than a polluted, liquefied roadway on which rode huge foreign tankers, garbage barges, speedboats, the yachts of the rich, and a few sailboats. Now I stand alongside Hell Gate, breathing the river into me, gazing at it, waiting for its turtles, geese, herons—the innocents we more often associate with Heaven's Gate. Thomas Berry, the eco-theologian and cultural historian, says that by pursuing what we love—our allurements—we help bind the universe together. Am I a madwoman now to think, like Maxey, that my allurement for the river might help her call in her creatures?

As a tugboat chugs down the river, I see a cormorant sitting on a dilapidated pier. It's not far from where I recently saw a snapping turtle swimming close to the surface of the water and almost mistook it for a deflated, discarded soccer ball. The cormorant extends his black wings to dry in the sunlight, and from the back looks much like the silhouette of Dracula. I watch him and remember the time I spent three years ago traveling through the underworld of the East River's sister waterway: the Arthur Kill. It is the place from whence the cormorant had flown, a place where all my ideas of nature as resplendent were abducted from me.

It is the faintest of sounds—a tiny *tic, tic, tic*—I hear as I hold to my ear an egg from which a seagull chick is pipping.

I am on the pebbly, scrubby, sandy shoreline of an island in the Arthur Kill—another large tidal strait in the Hudson estuary that runs through a polluted wetland along the western side of New York City's Staten Island, separating it from New Jersey. It is the end of my second summer as a volunteer assistant to two biologists for the Harbor Herons Project, and today we are searching for Canada goose nests. The search is a break in our usual routine of studying the more glamorous and elusive long-legged wading birds who, since the seventies, have made a miraculous comeback in the wooded interiors of isolated islands in the East River and the Arthur Kill.

As I place the seagull chick back into its nest on the shore, I silently laugh at myself for missing the messy research we do in the heronry. Going into the birds' seasonal nesting area as quickly and quietly as possible, we gently lift the baby birds from their nests in gray birches and quaking aspens to weigh and measure them. We handle just a small sample of the nestlings of the four thousand great egrets, snowy egrets, cattle egrets, little blue herons, black-crowned night herons, green-backed herons, yellow-crowned night herons, and glossy ibis who are living and raising their young quite invisibly within the boundaries of New York City. We count how many young are born and how many fledge. The birds are what is called an "indicator species"—as they are at the top of the food chain in their environment, their health indicates the health of the estuary.

reversing the tides

Across from the heronry and the seagull nest, on the New Jersey side of the Kill, the giants of the oil and chemical companies—DuPont, CITGO, American Cyanamid, Exxon, and others—make house. Their huge white storage tanks stand silent in the tall, lime green salt-marsh grasses, while their smokestacks spew out EPA-approved amounts of waste into the air over the marsh.

The history of the Arthur Kill, like that of the East River, should render it essentially lifeless from centuries of oil spills, raw sewage, and chemical dumping. The soft turf of the marsh has absorbed, and will continue to absorb, numerous oil spills that have caused the collapse of the fragile and already badly bruised ecosystem. Only recently has the Kill begun to bounce back. Still, when I glance down at my footprints in the sand I see oil that will persist for decades. It is buried but not benign.

I picture the mother herons fishing in the shallow depths of the Kill, their long bills poised to skewer fish, crab, shrimp: invertebrates who themselves have ingested the toxic and carcinogenic oils. The poison will be passed on, and in part explains why many of our nestlings fail to survive.

Scattered along the shore and hidden in the marsh grasses is a veritable Wal-Mart of used plastic products: empty plastic containers of dishwashing detergent, shampoo, yogurt, toilet-bowl cleaner, and Chinese takeout, as well as balls, toys, kitchen sinks, anything and everything I could ever imagine having in an apartment. The trash has slipped off garbage barges that every day carry more than ten thousand tons of New York City's trash through the New York Harbor and down the Arthur Kill to be dumped in the world's largest landfill that, as it happens, sits next to the heronry.

Not far from the hatching seagull are children's baby dolls. They dot the shoreline. One is stranded in the stark sunlight, half-buried in the sand with a hand in the air. Another is missing its eyes and a leg. A third is just a head. We are several women on this island investigating the birth of birds, and we are of course acquainted with dolls, symbolic plastic bundles of the life within us

—our own children, healthy, happy, living in a world abundant. But there is something sinister about the dolls' presence here, as though they are lost little ambassadors from the human world, living not in a foreign country but in humanity's damaged future.

On the days when our work with the baby herons is finished, we emerge from the heronry carrying an assortment of dog ticks on our bodies and splattered with what we call "splooj" (the word for the large and liquid bowel movements of baby birds), bird pee, and regurgitant (which is often a concoction of undigested invertebrates or, if it's that of cattle egret or black-crowned night heron mothers, maybe a few pieces of Kentucky Fried Chicken or a small mouse or two that mom plucked from the landfill).

But I also carry a gift: an intimacy with the spirits, sounds, and touches of birds. The snowy egret nestlings, so fearful even as I try to calm them, wrap their long reptilian-skinned toes around my fingers in an effort, I guess, to feel safe. The excruciatingly shy glossy ibis lay limp in my lap while I stroke their dark brown feathers. And although the black-crowned night herons assertively nip at me, I admire their aggressiveness; it helps them survive. The colors, habits, feathers, pecks, personalities, smells, movements, eyes, and cries of these birds are inside of me. I, quite simply, love them.

Tic, tic, tic. The seagull chick works tirelessly in the late morning sun to release itself. Using the powerful hatching muscles that run along the back of its neck and head, it is able to force a special egg tooth (a sort of temporary hatchet that has grown on the chick's upper mandible) against its beige and brown speckled shell to break it open—bit by bit by bit.

It is time to search for goose nests. As I gather up my binoculars and notebooks, I realize that after traveling through the Arthur Kill for two summers, I have given up trying to hate it. It both stuns and offends me. I cannot describe the chick's place of birth as ugly or beautiful: such labels seem too simple. I walk away from the chick knowing only that I feel deeply for this wasteland, where through the births of birds I've witnessed a kind of magic.

The tugboat on the East River sounds a loud honk to a passing oil freighter and the cormorant flies off to animate the sky. Another day and still no snapping turtle. Tomorrow I will wait again.

8 〔 My attachment to the East River has nothing to do with dipping my toes into it, with skipping stones over it, with riding it on an inner tube, with swimming it, with cooling my face with a splash of it, with walking along its shores, with even sitting close to it the way I imagine rural folk might do on lazy summer afternoons.

I feel sympathy for the East River, for everything it has lost, but I love it for the same reason I love the Arthur Kill: for its magic. In all their woundedness, these resilient waterways are managing to give life. I can't accept the injuries New Yorkers have caused this estuary, but I feel there's a need to cherish what is left.

Who knows, maybe when my father lifted me up on his shoulders all those years ago, my eyes focused not on the city, but on its surrounding dark and damaged olive green waters.

Off Being God

When I was a child, I spoke as a child, I understood
as a child, I thought as a child: but when I became
a man, I put away childish things.
I Corinthians 13

Three children who cannot sit still are about to take turns holding
Esther the barn owl. It is Birds of Prey Day at a school north of
Manhattan; and Esther, all of a pound heavy, will perch on the thin
arms of these children in front of an audience of hundreds gathered
under a big white outdoor tent. Esther will hold on with her four
powerful toes, two of which can turn forward and two backward. It
doesn't appear to matter to the children that soon their skin will
be lightly pricked with the weapons of an owl's body—the long,
curved, knife-sharp talons at the ends of Esther's toes, talons she
uses to snatch rodents, bats, and birds out of life, talons that plunge
into the torso of a mouse and pin it to the forest floor, enabling Esther to make the fatal bite at the base of the mouse's skull with the
other knife of her body, her sharp, hooked beak. The children are focused simply on holding Esther, whispering to Esther. And Esther,
sleepy Esther—the white feathers of her heart-shaped face rousing
beside the round and dimpled cheeks of these kids—will listen in-
tently with her asymmetrical skull, one ear-opening nearer the top
of her head than the other; but she will say nothing.

Usually, on a bright sunny morning such as this, when Esther
was wild, she would be sleeping just about now—in an old building, an attic, a cemetery, a church steeple, a barn—and so there is

no reason to change her ways and divulge the intricacies of meaning in what she says most often, which is not a hoot but a loud and scary-sounding *shreeee* screamed in flight. It is perhaps because of this dead-of-night habit of hers, this screaming in flight, along with her pale face and silent flying, that some call her species the ghost owl.

But facts are not concerns of the children. They, instead, are awash with the contentment that floods the body when one is considered by the dark eyes of a wild animal, an animal that seems in some way to be peering at and thinking of you. And if they are the eyes of a powerhouse animal, like a raptor, like Esther, and if you know—as the parent of a child who is about to hold an owl might —that with Esther's not inconsiderable strength she could rip the muscles out of your hands, it could be that the contentment felt in the presence of a barn owl is that brought on by what seems like the owl's compassion for your weaknesses: owl as the all-merciful.

Children in the audience, children who are not students of the school, yell out: "Can I hold Esther!?" "How many children does Esther have?" "How old is Esther?" "Please, please, I want to hold Esther!" In what they understand as their own bird sign language, the children prop out their black and white arms, stiff as branches, ready and willing for Esther to fly their way. None of the adults, including myself, hold out our metaphorical limbs. We, instead, are tree stumps. As much as there might be a desire to hold an owl, such childish, obvious enthusiasm was abandoned long ago. I suspect we stole it from ourselves, buried it like dogs do bones in the yard, thinking we'd get back to it when we had the privacy, the time, and the energy to chew on our emotions, when we had the guts to love animals the way children do: unashamedly, fearlessly, joyously.

I feel the need to dig up my bones while I am here, at Birds of Prey Day.

After Esther's show under the big white tent, a naturalist gives a short lecture about the lives of raptors and about why some species are declining. Pesticides and toxins in water and on croplands enter the foods raptors eat: rodents, fish, small birds, and amphibians; eventually the toxins build up in the raptor, killing, if not the bird itself, the bird's ability to reproduce. Then, we have habitat loss, occurring at dizzying speeds. Next, the incidentals: power lines that electrocute birds, glass buildings into which birds crash, and, not to be forgotten, says the naturalist, the general inhumanity of humans. "We shoot. We trap. We do," he says, "the expected, deplorable things."

Shaded under smaller gray tents are falconers eagerly awaiting to introduce us to their world, where rule little perched gods of grace and speed: gyrfalcon; peregrine falcon; goshawk; Harris hawk. Most of the birds' heads are covered with tiny elegant leather hoods that are, essentially, sophisticated blindfolds used to keep the birds sitting quietly. Their legs are secured, to either the falconer or to the perch, with leather straps and leashes; and hanging near each perch of each bird are things like hawk bells, tail bells, field leashes, and lures (the term for fake prey). With all the fancy gear and get-ups, with all the doting, the scene under the gray tents is much like a dog or cat show. Except every now and then, to calm a bird, a falconer gently strokes or shushes it—*shshhh, shhh, sh, sh*—with a respectfulness less commonly seen toward domestic animals. It is this relationship between falconer and raptor that in some ways is more intoxicating to witness than the actual flight of raptors chasing after lures. For it is not beyond imagining such a marvelous and powerful bird bonded instead to you, a bird flying from your fist and then returning from the wind, bearing its own mystery, and evoking in you the not so radical idea that this creature is some incarnation of the Divine.

Where the falconry tent ends, just by the bulging roots of an old oak tree, I see a large crowd gathering around the raptor I think of as ceaseless in my life: red-tailed hawk; and suddenly it is not as Rilke wrote, not "everything is far and long gone by." Since living in New York City, I have missed red-tailed hawks from the fields of my long ago, when we raced—I running along the country roads, they gliding the airstrips above. I remember the crayfishy smell of the creek under the one-lane bridge, near where foxes ran: this was where I found, anchored by its shaft in the sandy mud of the creek bank, a red-tailed feather leaning in the breeze. A friend of mine, an urban park ranger in New York City, once guided me to Inwood Park and to Central Park, close to the apartment of Woody Allen— the Woody Allen who said, "Nature and I are two"—who has had red-tailed hawks nesting near his lovely balcony. I've seen this pair perched behind the Metropolitan Museum, devouring blue jays for dinner. And finally, always like peacefulness coming, has been the red-tailed hawk of my dreams, the raptor who when I am chased in dark woods, hooks my shoulders with her talons and carries me under her lush and rust feathers to the top of a tree.

Are there people in the crowd, I wonder, digging up their own bones?

No matter what, a red-tailed hawk is the classic hawk, the quintessential of all magnificent soaring hawks. Undemanding— this could be said of a red-tailed, or extremely adaptable. The most recent generations of red-tailed hawks have grown up with me, or, more accurately, have grown again in numbers as I have grown. When I was born, a red-tailed hawk was rare, persecuted by environmental toxins that over the decades were outlawed. Now, some forty years later, red-tailed hawks are ubiquitous, the common roadside hawk perched along interstate medians, or, glance up, one is above you, kiting—which means hanging motionless on four-foot wingspans—over cornfields, housing developments, forest edges, and elementary schools while they hunt. A red-tailed commonly soars at five hundred to a thousand feet, viewing, from those heights, twenty-seven to thirty-nine square miles of the earth's surface. Which might make unsurprising the fact that one hawk can spot another from seven miles away. It would not be unusual to think of a red-tailed hawk as a witness to the many lives below: humans lounging in lawn chairs, shoveling snow, or taking an after-dinner walk; and as a witness, as well, to the smaller, quieter lives: mice and rats running in cornfields and parks; squirrels burying acorns; cottontails; starlings and sparrows flitting from bushes; pigeons cooing. Actually, it would not be terribly inaccurate to say red-tailed hawks are, if not omniscient, then, omnipresent.

The crowd around the hawk does not let up. Somewhere through all the questions, I hear the falconer say the hawk's name is Majestic. I decide to wait for the crowd to dissipate, realizing I finally will meet the species of bird that, in a certain sense, gave me back my voice last summer.

It was August in Cleveland, and I had flown in from New York to cover a story about Timmy, a gorilla who many Clevelanders believed was in love with another gorilla named Kate. The issue brewing about the gorillas was the imminent decision by zoo officials to move Timmy to a zoo in New York City, where, officials believed, Timmy ultimately would have a better and more prosperous conjugal life, a sort of multiple-choice life, with several female gorillas living in the Bronx Zoo. The ever-changing story of Timmy led the local evening news in Cleveland. Radio shows discussed the brouhaha. Local newspaper editorials rehashed the particulars. Kate, the story went, had brought Timmy out of the emotional shell in which he'd been trapped since his capture in the jungles of Africa decades ago. In a way that no other female gorilla could—and there had been several previous females—Kate had healed a deep trauma in Timmy's life. The problem was, Kate was not making more gorillas. And so after much deliberation zoo officials finalized the paperwork: Timmy would, for the good of the species, be moved to New York. This decision only served to light bigger fires of concern, the epitome of which came in the form of a letter to the public claiming to have been a letter from Timmy himself. Eventually, the two sides landed in court. That the issue had gotten this far distressed zoo officials because it proved, obviously quite well, that the masses, out of their deep regard for animals, could come together and nearly topple a couple of heretofore well-established authorities on nonhumans: the Cleveland and the Bronx zoos.

off being god

I recount all this to show that there was, undoubtedly, an animal vibe in Cleveland at the time; and unless you were, say, under eight years old, the conflict, and the questions it raised, were inescapable. It was not so much, Could animals love? Could they feel? Could they experience longing?, though of course those things factored in. Instead, the overarching question was more an issue of humans having dominion over these gorillas, of our playing God in their lives, of our subduing and controlling their fate. Who, after all, were we to say that the ability of two gorillas to be fruitful, or not, should be the deciding factor in their lives? What was, or should be, our relationship to them? Granted, the talk was of gorillas, nonhumans very similar to humans. But it was not unthinkable that such ideas—since they were so consistently and heavily argued—could be debated about animals in general: the squirrels in Cleveland Heights, say, or the robins in Shaker Heights, the foxes and coyotes near Chagrin Falls.

Or red-tailed hawks in median strips of major highways, on any day, or on the Sunday I saw one, on my way to church. This came about because I had decided to forgo staying at a hotel while on assignment and to bunk, instead, with my friends C and M. And on this particular day, C, who was a Catholic feminist, asked M and me to attend a charismatic Episcopalian liturgy at her church. I had not been in a church in years, so long that my mother, back in the Washington, D.C., suburbs, joked that the next time I stepped into a church either lightning would strike or the church would fall down. At any rate, M agreed, and so I would tag along too, for the experience. An experience, C said, that would be a welcome relief from the structured and controlled grip of the traditional Catholic Church. C said we would sing Christian light-rock, and dance. She assured M and me that charismatic worship was a "gentle, healing, freeing, and intimate way to expand one's relationship with God."

And so, as I remember, the conversation on the drive to church veered, in a roundabout way, to Nietzsche's thoughts about organized religion. Did it impose a herd mentality? A fixed order on the world? Was the human spirit repressed in its negation of instinct and passion in favor of reason and intellect? And what, by the way, did people see in their minds when they thought of God? Where was God?

We were talking cautiously, in the way friends must when speaking of religion, when I glanced out the car window and saw the red-tailed hawk in the median strip, mantling over, I guessed, a field mouse just caught.

"Did you see that hawk!?" I interrupted. They had not, and we kept driving.

We arrived at the church, which looked like a large, contemporary white house on the outside and, inside, like the top deck of a cruise liner, on the bow, where rows of chairs and benches provide vacationers the opportunity to stare into the flood of thought that oceans inspire. The simplicity of the interior, with several large beams running across the ceiling, reminded me of my vision of Noah's Ark, wherein Noah saved animals no matter their state of cleanliness. His story, it seemed to me, spoke through the power of metaphor to the idea of preserving nonhumans regardless of their usefulness to humans.

Before long, two hundred or so upper-middle-class parishioners, fairly underdressed, gathered on the bow in small groups to sip coffee, eat pastries, and discuss events of the past week. There seemed not a frown in the place. After patting the cinnamon and sugar from our mouths and crumpling our napkins, we took our seats across from a low stage that had upon it the altar and a large cross. There were no stained-glass windows, no flower arrangements, no dust, no incense, no pews, no Bibles. I tried to remember that C had said it would be this way, that there would be an ease here, an unfamiliar environment for the hard work of religion.

On our fold-up seats were photocopied pamphlets detailing the morning's agenda, as well as a few pages of lyrics. Three priests would manage the meeting, though Father Charles would lead. There would be the possibility, my neighbor whispered, that "people would be moved to speak in tongues or drop to the floor from the warmth of God's love entering their bodies." At other services, this woman continued, "people felt free enough to call out, to pray aloud, to soliloquize." This seemed fair; everyone would have the chance to be heard. During the next ninety minutes all these events did indeed occur. Though I admit to having snickered as discreetly as possible at the *Homo neanderthalensis*–like murmurings going on around me, and at the sudden falls to the carpet, I took the preaching seriously. For it was the preaching that, in the past, had been the bottleneck to believing.

Father Charles read and discussed several ideas before he began reading from Genesis: "And God said to them, Be fruitful and multiply, and replenish the earth, and subdue it: and have dominion over the fish of the sea, and over the fowl of the air, and over every living animal that moveth upon the earth."

This, I thought, might be a somewhat involved or messy passage for the day, given the state of things in Cleveland at the time. But there were no rebuttals in this court, no questions, no discussion. I wanted Father Charles to discuss the implications of moving, or not moving, beyond the typical interpretation of this passage, which is that of humankind as ruling master, and nature as slave. What, for instance, may have been lost in the translation from the Hebrew to English? And what might be the contributions of the expressions of the Psalms? Psalm 104: "You laid the earth's foundations so that they would never be destroyed. . . . May all selfishness disappear from me, and may you always shine from my heart." If Father Charles were to leap forward, to the New Testament, to the Resurrection, what could it mean that Jesus was mistakenly taken for a gardener? For was he not always a gardener and all that being a gardener implies, for humans as well as nonhumans: tending, replenishing, creating, and re-creating?

"Praise the Lord!" someone called out.

"Holy be the Lord!" another answered.

The passage apparently was accepted by citizens in a city that, at the time, was embroiled in questioning the human relationship to the nonhuman. Father Charles did not seize the opportunity to discuss the idea of preservation. He simply steered his ship through the same old waters, reminding me of a preacher Emerson described in *The Divinity School Address*: "He had no one word intimating that he had laughed or wept, . . . had been commended, or cheated, or chagrined. If he had ever lived and acted, we were none the wiser for it. The capital secret of his profession, namely, to convert life into truth, he had not learned."

Was this apparently fixed and unassailable thinking of Father Charles the crux of Nietzsche's concerns? Where was the wisdom of St. Augustine, the Christian theologian who said, "If you have understood, then this is not God. If you were able to understand, then you understood something else instead of God. If you were able to understand even partially, then you have deceived yourself with your own thoughts."

What if God *is* the hawk, *is* the fish of the ocean, the fowl of the air, and every living thing that moveth upon the earth? What if God *is* the grass the hawk sat in and the breeze the hawk flew through?

That I was a just a visitor to this church and unaccustomed in such environments to voicing questions—these should've been reasons to remain hushed and save my seat on the ship's bow. But I began feeling what I'd been warned I might: an unstoppable spirit and its concomitant urge to soliloquize oozing from my gut. It stumbled over my ribs, choked in my throat and loudly pushed through to Father Charles: *If you rule something, if you rule the earth, how can you love it!?* I yelled out.

Father Charles raised his hand toward me like a captain guarding a child running too close to the ship's safety rails: No walking beyond this point! Stop! And so this ark had sunk, and left me floating for a sense of the spiritual life.

Not long after, while everyone but C, M, and me was in line for communion, a woman bent down to me and, with a sudden and forceful hug, exclaimed, "Pray with us, honey!"

At the end of the service, just as we were heading for the door, a woman seized us and said, "Please come back. All your questions will be answered."

off being god

Since she was offering, I could not resist: "How," I said to her, hopefully, "would you answer my question?"

"The Lord knows best!" she said, breezing away, smiling.

Though C, M, and I knew that on our drive home the hawk would no longer be where it had been, we could not help looking for it out the window. Of course it was gone, somewhere, off being God.

Most of the crowd around Majestic is gone. I walk toward her realizing that, prior to Cleveland, I arrogantly assumed that the environment could be saved with the panoply of laws and research available to scientists and the government. These were the educational, rational, logical tools I believed could be used to persuade people of the severe and urgent needs of the planet. But since Cleveland, I had floated to shore, so to speak; and without all the baptismal water in my eyes, it was clear that it would not take more science but a new kind of religion—Christianity reenvisioned, reimagined, reinvented—to supplant the idea that humans stand in a special relationship to God, separating and elevating us from all that is nonhuman.

So I walk toward Majestic as a spiritual gypsy, which is to say I go to her as the children went to Esther.

"May I touch her?" I ask her falconer. I want the privilege of skin against feathers.

"Sure, she loves to be touched," says the falconer.

I move my hand down her ivory-feathered chest, the source of her winged power, and stroke her clove-colored wings held tight against her body. She rouses slightly, stands tall, and tips her head back and to the right to look at the sky out of her left eye. When she turns her head back to the falconer, her gold eyes catch me for a second before she's on to more interesting things—sparrows in trees, other raptors around her, the dog trotting by. I can't seem to stop touching Majestic; and as long as she approves I continue devoting myself to this bird in a way that must look like childish fascination.

"To become fascinated is to step into a wild love affair on any

the hopes of snakes

level of life," Thomas Berry, the eminent cultural historian, once said. Is this feeling, this fascination, this devotion, this wonder, this love affair with a red-tailed hawk, a way to begin feeling religious again?

Religion. The origin of the word is from the Latin *religare*, meaning "to bind." Maybe religion is like a dog digging up its bones in the yard, coming to that which it loves and barking with rapture, with gratitude, for it. Perhaps religion continues through the ecstatic binding between the dog and his beloved object of devotion—between dog's paws and bone, between dog's teeth and bone, between dog's tongue and bone, between dog and his entire focus on bone, bone, bone.

Religion, you ask? Bark, with gratitude, like a dog. Call out like a heretic. Beg, and keep begging: "Please, please, I want to hold Esther!"

The City's Laughter

It is hard to set nature apart in the city,
and everything, inside and out, takes on
the frame of a relentless housekeeping.
Elizabeth Hardwick

A city mouse dusted with the ancient soot of Manhattan runs across a sidewalk that, should the mouse decide to follow me, would lead the two of us to hundreds of mice playing in the train tracks of the Astor Place subway stop near where I attended graduate school in Greenwich Village, and where, in philosophy class, my professor once declared: "New York City is Nature! Capital *N!*" This was not the first time he'd emphasized a word in such a way. Actually, he preferred not to use the word *nature* and asked us to excuse him when he found it necessary to fall back on it, believing, as he did, that its use set up a dualistic way of thinking about the world: nature versus culture, that is. Which is a similar line of thought to that of Native Americans, who flourished not in nature, per se, but in a world of beings, of subjects, in a landscape of spirits, entities: others and self as part of a vast and exquisitely related world community. Nonetheless, we understood that our professor's declaration and emphasis meant something akin to god with a capital *G* or love with a capital *L*: the real thing.

"Skyscrapers, Korean delis, miles of roads and highways, restaurants, apartment buildings, the subway system, the entire city—all of it," the professor continued, "an anthill!" Noticing our perplexed faces, he rubbed the white whiskers of his chin, somewhat irritated at what he sensed must be our ignorance or our close-mindedness, and asked: "Do you really believe you are separate from Nature? New York is no different from a community of ants. Anthills are small skyscrapers, the ants' social system is one of workers and leaders. How 'bout that?" We paused respectfully, then denied it— "Ants? Hey, who has seen an anthill lately? Nobody. Capital *N!*"

On my way to the subway station, I try picturing eight million ants, which is the human population of the city, though the image is interrupted by several extra-round roaches scurrying along concrete and under the bench that cradles a sleeping homeless man, while a bold mouse darts from the alley beside Mia Pizza on East Broadway, a slice of pepperoni dangling from its mouth.

It is imperative to stand at the very edge of the subway platform if you want to see subway mice. It's not a place I used to wait, out of the somewhat valid fear of being shoved into the tracks. But soon into my seven years of living in a sunny and charming shoebox on Manhattan's Upper East Side, I learned quickly to pick and choose between that which is and that which is, mostly, not true about New York. I learned, too, that the city had a way of speaking, and this changed what it was I began hearing and seeing. Distant dots of the subway's headlights shining down long black tunnels were, for instance, new stars in my life, only closer. For those a long time in New York, there is, I believe, truth to their claim of hearing the slight rumbling of the train's engine much before the headlights are spotted by the city's newer residents traveling the currents downtown to uptown or crosstown. Indeed, much of the initial joy of living in New York is sailing on these currents—by cab, train, bus, or foot—from one location to the next, one person to the next, one event to the next; and it is invigorating, salubrious, in a salty and rough, high-tide way. Actually, describing the city as one giant starfish—each borough a starfish's leg, each person one of the countless tiny tube feet moving independently beneath the legs of the starfish, and the entire organism constantly, almost happily, in flux, searching and devouring what is found along the seabed of streets—is not necessarily a silly analogy, though it might seem so,

the city's laughter

comparing something so obviously of nature to something so seemingly not nature. This, though, would be the professor's point—to see the surface but to know that, below, there is a force pulling in the opposite direction of what we might imagine. There is an undertow here, in New York City.

If you visit Manhattan and don't yet trust the guidance of your senses because of course you are bombarded as soon as you hit the streets—bombarded by the morning air of bus exhaust, freshly applied perfumes, and coffee and toasted, buttered bagels; by the afternoon sparrows nipping at your breadbasket at the café, cigarette smoke, and packs of private-school kids running you off the sidewalk; by the East River or Hudson River walkways edged, as they are, with speeding cars on one side and, in spring, splashes of delicious flowers on the other—then get away, go to a subway station to acquire a new sixth sense, which is possible if you watch the subway mice. They know. Even as they chase one another—wildly, playfully, as though popping out from under dirty tissues is popping out from under golden leaves of corn—they are on alert for the trains. A mouse's acute sense of hearing and sensitive whiskers are so finely attuned to their environment that they sense oncoming trains much before trains are seen by lesser mortals. Alongside the steel tracks of the subway are the scent tracks of mice, tracks they travel, bumping into each other, sniffing, jumping, and talking in high-pitched squeaks, which, if it is late at night and you venture close to the platform's edge, can be heard. Often, someone tosses a candy bar, a hot dog, or a doughnut into the tracks, and the mice jostle closer to the platform, where I wait for them—wait because who can resist looking into the black orbs of eyes that belong to mice, city mouse or country mouse? When suddenly the mice abandon the doughnut for no obvious reason and duck into darkness, the subway is soon to arrive. Think of it as learning a kind of subway ecology. Spying on mice—their patterns and their interactions in an environment of trains and trash—I'm tempted to believe that nature in a New Yorker's life certainly revolves around a

the hopes of snakes

story of diminishment. But it is also a story of perception: What might we see if we shine nature's spotlight into the city's blacker seas of outcasts—the mice, roaches, and pigeons?

In environmental philosophy, we read the thoughtful words of na- ture philosophers, as well as the more renowned Emerson and Thoreau. But it is *Practice of the Wild,* by Gary Snyder, that is surprising and is clearly the source of my professor's claim that New York is Nature, capital *N*: "Science and some sorts of mysticism rightly propose that everything is natural. By these lights there is nothing unnatural about New York City, or toxic wastes, or atomic energy, and nothing—by definition—that we do or experience in life is 'unnatural.'" But a question, he alludes, is not necessarily, What is natural? or, What is Nature? But, What is wild?

Wild, as one might assume, describes the red-tailed hawks living uptown near the Metropolitan. Wild might describe the woodsy Ramble in Central Park, where colorful migrant songbirds can be found passing through this homeland of pigeons, starlings, and sparrows. Of course, afternoons have been spent searching for such creatures, waiting for them to fly over the meticulously manicured Great Lawn near where Pavarotti has sung. All of that is the fancier face of nature in New York City, which makes it more difficult to swim in darker waters, to float by the exiled, to be buoyed by the outcasts.

This does not mean there are no outcasts where I used to live on the Upper East Side, in the grander zip codes of 10021 or 10128, though they are perhaps more efficiently exterminated and, overall, less noticeable than the mice and rats daring daylight downtown. Besides, other neighborhood treats serve as distraction: four-star restaurants, exceedingly fancy shops, museums, and so many fountains spouting crystalline water—fountains in the circular driveways of expensive buildings, fountains in front of museums, fountains in playgrounds. It is as though whales swim below us; and, I imagine, the fountains are where whales surface to send up their steam. Then, in springtime, the thousands and thousands of pink, yellow, orange, and lavender tulips like exotic tropical sea-shells washed up in the median strip of Park Avenue.

My old apartment, in a building off Second Avenue, was far away from any whales and seashells. Still, it could be described as charming, which means outrageously small, maybe four hundred square feet, and, usually, sun-filled, which made up for the small-ness. It was a quality-of-life issue: sunlight, considered so valuable in Manhattan as to be a completely acceptable reason to hike up the rent. Proximity to sunlight is another way New York speaks, and it alters not only how you see and hear but, more importantly, how you feel. This is said with some degree of experience, having lived, like many New Yorkers, in a dark cavern or two.

The rental of my first cave, on Thirty-fourth off Park, cost $1,000 for the one month my boyfriend and I survived it. Roaches lived in the cracks behind the toothbrush holder tiled into the wall, roaches crawled on the toilet seat, they slept in the plastic egg con-tainers on the door of the fridge. "All them roaches?" the superin-tendent laughed, walking away from me after I'd stopped him in the soot-stained hallway to complain. "Hell, girl, it's nature here. You from the suburbs, ain't ya?"

I was. I had naively rented the flat over the telephone, from my then home in the suburbs of Washington, D.C., where as an under-graduate I was used to paying $300 a month in rent. A thousand dollars—how elegant, sophisticated, and wonderful it must be, I thought. Talking on the phone, the rental agent suggested that the apartment resembled everything a Manhattanite dreams of: floor-to-ceiling bookcases with a sliding ladder in a goldenly lit li-brary, French doors, ample natural light, old wood floors, a fire-place, a separate kitchen, plaster rosettes centered in high ceilings. The word I missed in the conversation was *resemble*; neglecting, as the agent had, the truth that everything she described was what the building had looked like in its heyday.

On move-in day in December, my boyfriend and I drove along Thirty-fourth Street as *Miracle on 34th Street,* the only Thirty-fourth Street I knew, replayed in my mind. Crossing town, we passed

Macy's; the Salvation Army Santa Claus ringing his bells; and the sidewalk vendors selling roasted chestnuts, the smoke from which mixed in the air with car exhaust and the winter breathing of thousands of Christmas shoppers. When finally we pulled up to what I'd imagined would be my own "Edith Whartonian" row house, it was clear things would be otherwise. The building had indeed once been a single-family home, but somewhere along the way all exterior details had been painted over in a dull gray. The main floor living room window was now the window of a liquor store, and, out front, splashed on the pavement, were men who were not Jimmy Stewart. This would not be our beautiful house.

Things picked up when, inside the apartment, I noticed a high ceiling with a centered plaster rosette; but a switch of the light revealed hundreds of roaches enjoying the high ceilings themselves. After the first week of job searching during the day and "Raid-ing" at night, we stored all our food and utensils in plastic bags and sat with our legs crossed and up off the floor. After two weeks, we gave up, stayed out all day, ate out for every meal, and returned at night to the walls of our battleground, walls that appeared to move with battalions of roaches. Nothing we did helped us win the daily war, and so at bedtime I pulled out the only ammunition I had left: long underwear and socks, cotton stuffed in my ears, and my boyfriend, atop of whom I slept all night, as though on a two-by-four over water. I moved out wondering if these roaches were in fact nature or the wild gone, in a way, AWOL. In other words, something natural was absent from where it should be, where it once was, but not all parties were intent on deserting completely.

For the longest time there were no roaches in the apartment we later came by, the sunny, charming, shoebox apartment. But as time passed we noticed what New Yorkers euphemistically call "transients." These are roaches that are passing through your place (you are completely convinced despite any hard evidence, which, after all, you have no interest in gathering) on their way to someone else's, someone who is messier, smellier, an Oscar instead of a Felix.

the city's laughter

My friend on Madison Avenue had these transients, though she called them "water bugs." It's a form of denial that sounds better to guests when, on a trip to the loo during your elegant dinner party, they see a brown, leathery, oval-shaped . . . arthropod! . . . moving across the floor and return to the table unexpectedly soon. The going knowledge on the subject is: if you have rather large transients then you don't have roaches; but if you see tiny roaches then you have baby roaches and, alas, you therefore have roaches for real.

Cockroaches—primitive and ancient—have remained virtually unchanged for some 300 million years. If they live their allotted lifespan of four or more years, females can produce more than a thousand eggs. Chances are excellent that she will produce her thousand children, due to the vibration-sensing organs nearly covering her body, organs that assist a roach in befuddling its human predators. Anyone who's tried killing a roach knows the intense frustration of getting just close enough and then, boom, missing the mark. This results in the diligent and patient practice of learning to approach a roach from just the right angle, all the while believing this tiptoeing onward toward the target and then hesitating at the slightest lull in the roach's movement is a roach's masterful harassment of humans. It's best, I know now, to storm in from the top by dropping something that, being heavy, moves fast.

I gleaned my roach anatomy trivia from another of my favorite professors—my animal-behavior professor—who, in her apartment across town on the Upper West Side, had been in the midst of performing her own private experiment to determine if roaches liked tuna or beer best, seeing, as she did, more roaches than usual on the mornings when dishes left overnight in the sink had upon them scrapings of tuna or the sticky film of beer. Because I truly considered her quite a brilliant woman—she could recall studies from obscure ethological journals, she could predict the outcomes of certain tests—I believed she was caught up in her own genius and in need of some common sense advice: *Perhaps washing the dishes would help,* I offered. But the situation presented itself as a fascinating and insistent question: beer or tuna, beer or tuna, which is best loved?

Repeated trials proved, come morning when results were tallied, that more roaches were stuck to the double-sided extra-strength tape on, as I remember, the beer bowl, which, we pondered, could be meaningful research for fraternity houses.

Eventually, my boyfriend and I decided we had roaches for real, and the source of the problem was a very old woman, the superintendent said, living directly two floors below us. She had yet to sign up for the monthly extermination service, and her roaches were multiplying furiously and crawling through the walls and pipes and floors up to us. It became necessary, therefore, to march downstairs, intending to demand of a woman I had never actually seen or met the acceptance of a service she had, in the past several months, at least, forgone.

I knocked on her bare brown door and knocked again, hard enough that the door rattled and I jumped back to remove myself from the dozens of roaches of all sizes and several varieties that seeped from the edges and scattered across the face of the door. Slowly, a lock was unlocked and unlocked and unlocked, the typical three or four locks on a New Yorker's door, and a woman in a nursing uniform answered sleepily. I peeked into the tiny place and saw an old, white-haired woman, her eyes buried beneath wrinkles, as she slept and wheezed heavily in the beige, dusty air of the place that smelled like trash and stale perfume.

"Can't sign up," said the nurse.

"Why?"

"Can't have that poison around . . . not good for her breathing," she answered, looking briefly at her patient. "She's almost dead," she added, dispassionately. "You know, she was born in this building, two floors up."

That would be my apartment, I wanted to say, but did not, realizing I was caught in the middle of two of nature's life forces: 300 million years of the paradoxically repulsive yet enduring roach; and three months or weeks or days or hours of what was left of the old woman.

Back upstairs, sitting in the sunny yellow light on my bed, I

the city's laughter

stared, hopelessly, at the roaches crawling up the steam pipe that ran inside the building; and I imagined the old woman as a baby brought home to this room, ninety-odd years ago, when the bathtub was still in the kitchen. I imagined the baby crying, imagined her growing and taking her first steps here until she became strong enough to run up and down five flights of stairs. I saw her playing in the sunny living room where my cats were lounging.

Then, in my own askew mind, in my own feelings of going AWOL, I guiltily wished the old lady would hurry up and die.

It's tempting to call them Pigeon Ladies, preferring, as they do, the friendship of pigeons that come to their soft, old bodies with the loyalty and discipline of homing pigeons coming home from wherever they may be in the city—on ledges, in ventilation holes, atop hard worn balconies and roofs. In warm weather, usually, pigeon ladies, and sometimes men, sit on park benches in modicums of quiet, where city sirens and horns are mere whispers through summer's leafy trees. A withered woman, her shoes hanging off her heels, taupe-colored knee-high stockings at her ankles, white legs bulging with blue veins, her drooping and torn brown coat, her shoulders teetering with pigeons, her gnarled hands stroking three cooing pigeons on her chest, while other pigeons hover around her, landing in and flying out of her ratty white hair teased into a cascading nest that drapes down her wrinkled and fair face—this vivid memory of a pigeon lady shot through me suddenly when, looking with my three cats out the window of my fifth-floor apartment, I noticed an elderly white-haired woman, with her cats, waving at me from the window of her fifth-floor apartment across the street. We met for the first time like this, with cats in sunlight, not knowing we would wave again and again for two years, not knowing we would come to look forward to the wave.

It's a habit I've had since childhood, gazing out windows. And when New Yorkers are acting like New Yorkers—which is not necessarily brash, mean, and underhanded, though there are sometimes those qualities—people-watching out your window carries with it the distinct possibility of lunchtime theater. Such was the case of the woman I came to call St. Francis, dressed in expensive black clothing, black pumps, a black leather briefcase, a black coat, and a folded black umbrella, which she carried on days it was not raining, leading me to assume she might use it for protection from the sun, which led to the further thought that she must be somehow fragile. In every way except perhaps the fragility, she was someone I would have expected to see on the Second Avenue bus heading to midtown on the way to work in the morning, when I was working, that is. But at the time I was in graduate school, and often I was home studying, which involved a certain degree of staring out the window. And so St. Francis walked down my street nearly every day over the period of six weeks or so, at lunchtime.

For some unknown reason, as my block had as many pigeons as any other block in Manhattan, this woman chose the sidewalk in front of my building as the perfect place to throw generous amounts of bird seed, for pigeons, I assumed. Although as I started to monitor Francis more vigilantly, it was not clear for whom the seed was meant. She did not stay and wait for birds to swarm her, as did other pigeon admirers readily available in the city, people I had once believed acted out of sympathy for the birds, as if in a just world even outcasts deserved something of our care. But I have watched, from old green painted park benches, pigeon people involved in more than sympathetic seed tossing. People, who, with gentle hands and warm chests, stroked their full-bodied, mild-mannered, and gentle-voiced pigeons, as though pigeon and person nourished each other, as though they understood each other's longings. Call it what you want, but consider: those believed to be sane among us show similar devotion to our dogs and cats. As domesticated pets do for domesticated people, wild pigeons do for wild pigeon people: make them happy. And peaceful, it seemed.

St. Francis, though, just threw and threw and threw, fistfuls of seed, quickly, and then, before pigeons swarmed down from their sooty, dark ledges, she left, her umbrella poking the concrete alongside her strident footsteps.

How kind, I thought, at first, when she began spreading her seed. Perhaps this was due to the fact that the seed drew to my old, black iron fire escape the pretty purplish-red-headed house finches, and, occasionally, the otherwise-located Central Park birds. But word spread among pigeons, as it will, and among rats, too. And so there were at this point kind requests from various people on the block that Francis stop what she was doing. Patient-sounding requests spoken haltingly and carefully, which is another way to describe New Yorkers, and how I most often think of them, as though we all lived, friendly and concerned, in a small village delineated by dry-cleaning establishments and Korean delis.

The requests to Francis sometimes worked, and a few days would pass without our urban saint. But she would return later in the week, the sound of her umbrella rapping the sidewalk. Until one man could no longer stand it and detailed for Francis the pigeon waste he walked through every day, not to mention the extra rats now vehemently riffling through our garbage cans. He demanded, loudly, meanly, and in her face, that she leave, find another sidewalk, maybe one in front of her building would be a good idea. This was when Francis finally spoke, in long breaths of gibberish, as she opened her black briefcase, pulled out her bag of seed and showered the man with a wild throwing.

This, anyone could see, was of course upsetting the man terribly. One might guess the man would retreat in the face of St. Francis's insanity. Instead, he became more agitated, trying to speak to a woman who could not speak to people; and all I could think of was how much Francis needed the pigeons she never waited for, the mild, soft pigeons this city offered, as refuge, as nature in its, if not wild, then outcast form.

The old woman in the fifth-floor apartment across the street has not waved in a couple of days, which is unlike her. Nearly every day for the past two years she has at some point during the day sat at the window, her five cats on or around her lap, watching me and my cats, or the street, or sky. This disconnected peering at each other has been our sole connection. Once, when she saw my calico jump up to usurp my Siamese from the coveted, southern-exposed windowsill, she opened her mouth in surprise and then pointed at her calico, as though we were living parallel lives.

It was now a week without the waving woman, and since I have not seen lights in her apartment at night, I surmise she has died, though I look for her over and over again. This is when, one afternoon, I see a pigeon thrashing against her window from inside her apartment and decide to go across the street and free the bird. It is easy, in our less-expensive buildings that have no doormen or guards, to buzz the intercom of a resident and claim you are the Chinese-food delivery person needing to be let in. This is what I do.

Her apartment door is open, swinging in a breeze originating inside. I walk in and am suddenly covered in pigeons, pigeons landing on my head, pigeons crashing into my chest and crawling up to perch on my shoulders. I hear the scuttle of their feet crossing the old wood floor and the cooing of those gathered around my legs. It is as though I'm a sculpture of some goddess they've been expecting. I shake them off. Pigeons, feathers, dust, bird excrement. Filth is everywhere, and I think, predictably, that this is what killed my old waving woman. In the living room—the room from where she sat and watched me—stained wallpaper hangs loose near the ceiling, which is cracked and which, in one corner, has opened into a hole in her roof, an entrance to the sky. On the floor underneath the ceiling sits a bucket partially filled with rainwater. In the hallway leading to her bedroom, an old gramophone and a stack of 33⅓ rpm records cover a table. Her mattress is folded on the floor. There is no bed frame; the bedroom window is shattered. I hear baby pigeons squealing, their unmistakable cries like ungreased wheels endlessly turning, and I follow the sound to the kitchen. Above the cabinets are pigeon nests. On the windowsills are pigeon nests. Every available ledge has upon it a pigeon nest. The woman has not been gone long enough for all of this to have taken place since her departure. She has been living, who knows how long, with dozens and dozens of pigeons, monogamous mates raising their young together—the male pigeon incubating eggs by day, the female by night—here in an apartment on East Seventy-third Street. The woman has slept alongside the secret births of pigeons, secret because the sight of baby pigeons in city streets is rare. Find your way back behind the fancy brownstones, row houses, and refurbished tenement buildings of Manhattan to the sooty, forgotten, and mostly inaccessible spaces of concrete, soil, bushes, and trees, and you will find the refuge of baby pigeons. They grow there, in the shadows of buildings, backstage, until they are strong enough to conquer New York. Conquer the skies with their powerful, skillful, and beautiful flying. Have you ever noticed sunshine glowing behind the feathers of a flying pigeon's outstretched wing, as though the bird rides sunrays? Bashful does not describe city pigeons, hovering, as they do, around your café table during alfresco luncheons. They know—from excellent vision inside their fiery eyes—where you are. Think of them as always watching. Think of their ardent coos as songs at the windowsill.

As I stand in the sanctum of this woman, among the hundred or so pigeons she once knew, I realize she was the memory of the woman in the park, she was the one with the cascading white hair and bulging blue veins. For my waving woman, nature, quite literally, meant an exquisitely related community consisting of herself and these birds. Pigeons meant home.

I imagine that in the weeks before the woman died, she held these baby pigeons, as well as broods from the months before, and those before them, nurturing generations, as would a grandmother. That she listened to the birds and knew something of their intelligence; that she witnessed their days, their flights to and from her roof; that she knew the intoxicating colors of the birds' flashy neck feathers—tropical garden green, cabernet red, turquoise blue; that she walked to the park and above her flew her birds, her cloud lined with silver wings, until she arrived at her bench, where birds landed in her lap—how could all this not have been?

the hopes of snakes

Manhattan. There are many languages spoken there. And though one of them is not "wildness" in the way it may typically be defined —as nourishing nonhuman diversity—there are, nonetheless, remnants, sparks, holdouts, representatives, entities, beings, subjects from the wild, species clinging to this landscape. The streets of New York City are not wild with a capital *W,* though perhaps wildness is seen mostly by those who behold it regardless of its beauty; by those attempting to reconcile the great loss of diversity in one moment and, in the next, praying that further development remains within the paved boundaries we already have constructed. Maybe it helps to imagine the city as a starfish, or to appreciate, on some level, the sensuality of pigeons, the eternity of roaches, the antics of subway mice. Maybe not. "Earth laughs in flowers," said Emerson. In Manhattan, perhaps Earth laughs, a bit sarcastically, in its dark, natural, and wild outcasts.

Snow Day

for Marisa

We were to have late-afternoon tea on Fifth Avenue, at The Pierre, one of Manhattan's classiest hotels, which serves its clientele in one of the city's foremost tearooms. We had been there before and knew that afternoon tea, and the sweets that came with it, required a kind of invisible, feminine way of eating, eating accomplished while speaking quietly, mysteriously, hushed, all proper and English-like, frosted with the air kisses of the French. We knew to expect classical music, to sit where we had sat before, in overstuffed tapestry-upholstered chairs, our legs daintily crossed, our bodies drenched by small clouds of smoke blown by rich ladies lunching. We would finger delicate sandwiches of cucumber and cream cheese, and colorful cookies and brownies and Belgian chocolates. These were the offerings we would make to our bodies, once we arrived.

But outside, on the windy streets, the orange sky of late October flung itself into dark corridors of the city, and into me, as I made my way to The Pierre. So though my friend was beautiful, walking to the corner to meet me, her hair a wild breeze of black curls, her loose paisley pants flowing like water down her legs, her shoulders warm inside a thick blue wool sweater, I knew I could not go for tea. When she stood beside me, smelling like a vase of apple cider, cinnamon, and lingering chimney smoke, all I could imagine was tilting our heads toward the falling sun and spilling our hair into leaves dropping in Central Park.

It was about this time we began listening to the deeper stirrings

34

of our bodies. Believing our fingers had a feeling for dangling through grass in Central Park's Great Lawn; believing our lungs could lure us to the cherry air blossoming around the reservoir; believing our spines ached to arch along the ancient gray boulders near Sheep Meadow; believing in the sparrow's music by the boat pond. In a city of wealthy and fancy kingdoms, we had inherited these smaller, richer delights of Central Park.

This is how, months later, we approached a threshold: the decision to cross the park's frozen lake one winter day, before we married our men and had our children. There was the scattering snow, like breathlessness, the rupturing wind, a lucid sky. We could love this. Now, still, we talk of that day, when the ghosts of our girlness led us across the ice and into virgin snow, where we spread our limbs in the powder and drew upon the earth our angels trapped inside. We, women, urban women, fell to the ground, silent, and swallowed the wet, cold earth that raised us, the sweet earth we otherwise might never again have tasted.

snow day

Heirloom

Thunder and lightning and stars and...flowers, birds,
animals, trees—all these have voices.... Somehow we
have become autistic. We don't hear the voices.
Thomas Berry

Although I knew it impossible, I asked for a feather anyway, specifically the brown feather from the peregrine falcon tethered on
her perch beside me and brushing my arm with her long, outstretched wing. "Possessing any body part of a peregrine falcon is
illegal," the falconer, Dr. Heinz Meng, sternly answered. "You
know that."

I did.

Still, I foolishly asked again, figuring a request for the small,
downy feathers that Janice, Dr. Meng's peregrine, had shed, and
which lay mixed with her sticky droppings below her perch, would
not be so sorely missed. He laughed, "No one's ever asked for those.
But...well...No!"

Feathers: the ultimate symbols of flight, of lightness and the
unrestricted power of transcendence. The red breast feathers of
robins scattered under leaves in woods. The yellow feathers of
finches in wild lupine. Blue jay's feather poking through pine nee-
dles. Sparrows' feathers floating in rain puddles. I spent my childhood perfecting the art of finding feathers in the way some people
concentrate their spare energy finding four-leaf clovers.

The primary flight feathers. The main coverts. The secondary
flight feathers. All were available and, once I had lifted them, were
stashed away in my small reproduction of a buried treasure box, the

kind children imagine are filled with jewels deep at sea and which I had, in fact, been given as a child. By the time I had asked Dr. Meng for the peregrine feather, I'd had the treasure box for twenty-five years, and it was nearly full.

As a kid, I took the feathers out of the box periodically, though not with the symbolic or romantic intentions of garnering transcendence or lightness. Life was not yet so weighted. My aim was much more simple and sensual. Through the feather I could stroke a small part of the bird's sleek, streamlined, silky body and imagine not myself but the *bird* in flight. Surely you know of children who have insatiable desires to acquire things that speak deeply to them: insects, or pictures of the moon, model airplanes, or dolls, or trucks. Maybe you were one of them; we all have something. For me it was feathers of suburban birds, a largely indistinct group of avians. Nevertheless, the fascination spread beyond finches and robins to the intelligent crow, the mysterious owl, and eventually—during a backpacking trip in Vermont's Green Mountains one summer with friends—to the mysterious peregrine falcon.

That summer, as I remember it, I approached a cliff near the top of a mountain, where a man appeared from behind the rocks to which we were headed. Amidst the high-pitched, insistent, and obstreperous *kek kek kek kek* calls of birds I could not see, the man said softly and protectively: "We are reintroducing peregrine falcons to these cliffs. You all will have to turn back."

Turn back? We had zig-zagged up and down several mountains and had become confident in the somewhat unearned way that high-schoolers believe themselves to be. We were, after all, close to the end of an adventure and had been surviving with only what we carried on our backs: food, a mildewed change of clothes, a couple rolls of toilet paper, a few pots, flip-flops, a sleeping bag, a hammock, and a dirty plastic tarp. We drank from streams and slept strung between trees in hammocks. We had learned to tell time from the sky and to smell rain before it arrived. Our hair was greasy, and our fingernails weren't too pretty, either. A bath? That was two weeks ago, when we'd started; and now the Pop-Tarts were

heirloom

gone and we were on our last bites of the inch-thick salami sticks we carried in our pockets. Our mission was to successfully cross part of the mountain range, not go back. And so, being young and believing that the world, and at that moment the Green Mountains, belonged to us, we refused to turn back.

Things changed quickly when other men wearing badges and carrying impressive-looking electrical and photographic equipment came to assist the first man, who subsequently identified the situation as important ornithological research and then, more authoritatively this time, explained that we had no choice: "You must turn back."

We marched away, defeated and unaware that at that time, in the mid-1970s, DDT and other related pesticides had decimated America's population of peregrine falcons. The biologist's captive-bred peregrines were part of an enormous effort to restore the falcon to the eastern United States. I hiked down the mountain scanning the ground for a feather different from all those I'd had at home in my treasure box—a feather that might belong to the peregrine I'd not even seen. And I eavesdropped on the sky, hoping on an off chance to trace the voice I had heard coming from behind the rocks to the flying body of this elusive yet clearly very important bird, not knowing it would be decades before I again would be this close to a peregrine.

"The feathers are lovely though, aren't they?" said Dr. Meng, as he carried Janice out of her mews, toward the lawn, where he placed her on a low perch close to the ground. "Sit with Janice a while, if you like," he said, as he walked into his house to finish some paperwork. Fastened to her perch with leather jesses, which were like leashes around her legs, Janice preened, stretched her wings, and stared into the surrounding trees where sparrows, robins, and house finches darted by, perilously close to her. The small birds seemed to know that, for Janice, wild prey—them, specifically—was an impossible delicacy.

Janice, not much larger than a crow, lightly fluttered her brown, tan, and ivory feathers against the spring grass. If Janice lived in New York City, where I had lived, and where wild peregrines rule the sky like lions rule the savannah, she would hunt pigeons, quick and powerful birds in their own right. With eyes eight times more powerful than a human's, Janice would spot a pigeon as far as a mile 39 away before diving after it "like a feathered bomb," Dr. Meng had said. Peregrines are built for speed with streamlined heads and a specialized nostril that slows the rapid river of air that otherwise would flood into them when they fold their wings and transform into the shape of a bullet traveling up to two hundred miles per hour. Gravity adding a terrific power to Janice's skull-splitting blow, she would strike her airborne victim with her sharp talons, the impact sounding like a punching fist, stunning the pigeon before she would sever the cervical vertebrae with her beak, finishing her kill. Janice: a peregrine falcon: a perfect predator.

But none of this was going to happen while secured to her perch. Oh, to be free, to be the brutal poetry of the air—these were Janice's desires, I guessed, watching her watch the backyard birds; and her endlessly shrill and rapid *kek kek kek kek kek!* was how she alarmed the world to her presence.

Falco peregrinus. Falco comes from the Latin *falx* or "sickle," which describes the bird's sickle-like talons and beak. *Peregrinus* is Latin for "wanderer." Sickles that wander. A partial list of the peregrine's assorted common names shows that it occupies the world: *wanderfalk, slechtvalk, faucon perelin, pelligrino, sokol, shaheen, kidgavitch, kiriat, halcon pollero.* Peregrines live on every continent except for Antarctica and have inhabited virtually every language since ancient times. The Egyptians, for example, believed that the peregrine, flying at dawn and dusk, assisted the sun in rising and setting each day.

The summer after I met Dr. Meng, I waited through late afternoons for a pair of peregrines to fly the sun down behind the building that is now the New York Presbyterian Hospital–Cornell University on Manhattan's Upper East Side, where the birds live.

The hospital's sky-scraping stone walls resemble the peregrine's ancestral cliff dwellings; the city's resident pigeons, as well as birds that migrate along the Atlantic flyway during spring and fall, are their ample food source. Far below the nest, in the hospital's parking lot, I fixed my binoculars on what I'd come to imagine as an inner-city cliff near the East River, one of fifteen sites that monogamous pairs of wild peregrines occupy within the five boroughs of New York City.

One of the few people to climb the heights of each peregrine nest site is Chris Nadareski, who took me on unofficially as a graduate student assistant. A wildlife biologist who studied under Dr. Meng, Chris is the research scientist and supervisor of wildlife studies for the New York City Department of Environmental Protection (NYCDEP). He is quick to remark that "the peregrines help maintain an ecological balance in the city, even though it's so far out of whack in so many ways. If, at the top of the food chain, they're successful, we know that the ecosystem is working at the lower levels." His love and enthusiasm for the peregrines are contagious. Chris is a man who, upon seeing a pair fly into their nest, will explain and imitate the birds' behaviors for the curious onlooker: "*Eee-chup, eee-chup* is what they're saying. Now see them bow," he says as he squats and bows. "They're preparing for their courtship rituals." An explanation like this casts a sort of peregrine love-spell over many people who manage the city's famous buildings and bridges where the peregrines nest. They may get the species wrong ("Hey, Chris, how's those eagles?"), but they're nevertheless protective and proud of their wild penthouse charges.

Chris monitors the falcons throughout the year since, unlike most North American peregrines that travel to South America for the winter, the New York City population remains home. New York winters are not severe enough to force the falcons out, and the endless supply of pigeons keeps them well fed. Spring and summer, when the birds breed and raise their young among skyscrapers, helicopters, and humans, are Chris's busiest times of year.

In late spring, Chris bands each nestling with an identification anklet that instructs anyone finding an injured or dead peregrine to contact the U.S. Fish and Wildlife Service (USFWS). During the banding sessions at the peregrines' nests, the parent birds, who understandably abhor the removal of their young, attack Chris, which is why he wears a motorcycle helmet and a thick, full-bodied construction suit to climb to the nests. The attire protects him as well as the birds that, during an attack, could tangle their talons in Chris's loose hair, his wristwatch, his belt, anything. He prefers that the birds simply make a quick, clean hit on him.

The first captive-bred peregrines flew to New York city in 1983, after being raised by Dr. Meng and others, and were released into the wild by the same biologists I had come across in the mountains of Vermont in the mid-1970s. A decade later, by May 1993, nine pairs of the New York City peregrines had had their most successful breeding season. Thirty-five young were born, though by mid-October eight young were confirmed dead and two were missing. In any year "certainly some young will be successful," said Chris, "and others just won't be. Some starve to death not only here at their breeding grounds but during the time they spend looking for their own new territories. They may run into a tremendous amount of trouble, mostly from humans, whether directly or indirectly through construction, power lines, or skyscraper windows they mistake for the sky and try to fly through." In spring of 2003, twenty years after the birds' arrival, nine pairs of falcons laid eggs; and out of those, six pairs became happy parents, giving the world seventeen new falcons.

Peregrines prefer open skies in the way whales prefer open oceans, space through which they can move unimpeded, sinuously. But because the birds nest on sheer rock walls, they've adapted, over the decades, to living among the skyscrapers of North American cities. Before Chris's peregrines arrived in the Big Apple, a peregrine pair twice tried to nest atop the St. Regis Hotel in Manhattan in the 1940s, but both times were forced out by human interference. Philadelphia's City Hall in the 1940s and a church steeple in Harrisburg, Pennsylvania, in the 1950s each welcomed a

pair of falcons. However, by the late 1950s and early 1960s peregrines were disappearing in the eastern United States due to the
widespread effects of DDT and associated pesticides.

By 1972, North America and most European countries had restricted or outlawed DDT and other suspected killer organochlo-
rines, such as aldrin and dieldrin. "But," said Chris, "we're certainly
not free of the problem by any means. It's a very persistent substance." For instance, Venezuela, which in the past has received
large shipments of DDT, is one of the main wintering spots for the
more than two hundred migrant North American bird species that
visit us during the spring and summer in our parks, backyards,
woodlands, and grasslands. Some of those species summer in New
York City's Central Park, continuing the cycle of poison when a
peregrine eats a migrant.

After banding the New York Presbyterian Hospital nestlings, we
headed south to a nest near Grand Central Station, in midtown,
atop the towering MetLife Building that cuts Park Avenue in half.
In wilderness areas, peregrines nest on the edges of cliffs inaccessible to humans and lay their eggs in what is called a "scrape"—a
simple depression in the rock. In the city, the NYCDEP assists the
birds by building, on skyscrapers and bridges, scrapes made of ply-
wood, boxes that open to the sky on one side.

A service elevator took us to the top of the MetLife Building,
where we walked out into the sky. At the scrape on the northern
side of the building, Chris pulled out three round, three-week-old
chicks, snowballs of downy feathers. They rolled awkwardly on
their bottoms, flinging forward their light yellow, reptilian-like
feet. While Chris banded the babies, the parent peregrines circled
us, calling loudly: *kek kek kek kek!*

If you had been there, nearly sixty stories above Manhattan, you
would have noticed several things. For example, the wind whip-
ping around the skyscraper and the apparent ease with which it
could flick you to the street. And you would see a landscape beyond
Manhattan, a terrain of waters—the Hudson River, the East River,

the Atlantic Ocean, the bays—and greener, wider land. On a clear day you would look through the open skies to the Palisades of the Hudson River—sharp gray cliffs where wild peregrines nested decades ago. If your eyes followed the Hudson River south to its confluence with the East River, you would see olive green bay water surging into the Atlantic. The fetid smell of the city's summer streets, so redolent of trash and human urine, would vanish in the winds. In fact, the city below you would almost disappear. Given the opportunity to look beyond the familiar concrete scenery, you could, with this temporary reprieve from the purely urban, imagine the island of Manhattan three centuries ago, thickly forested and ringed with lime green marshland. Meanwhile, the MetLife peregrines would keep circling you, assessing you, calling to you: *kek kek kek kek*. Assuming you would welcome it, the mantra of the falcon would rap in your head and slowly you would sense yourself entering, or at least reaching, into something wild, something your body senses, responds to, knows. Some border would have been erased and the world of the peregrine and its life would be ripping in you.

Chris worked quickly but gently on the three nestlings. He secured a black and red USFWS band to one leg of each bird; he misted lice spray under the bird's wings; he checked the insides of the bird's mouth with a small flashlight. And *voila*. Next.

Before returning the babies, Chris cleaned the nest-box, in which he found a piece of wing from a cedar waxwing, several regurgitated pellets of undigested bones and feathers, a blue jay's head, and an unidentifiable piece of another bird. A few peregrine feathers blew out with the decaying body parts; and although I knew it was illegal, I considered scooping them up. But with another gust of wind the feathers floated off the roof, destined for the city streets below where they would be mistaken for pigeon feathers, if they were noticed at all; and I felt seized then by what could not be seen or touched: the peregrine's call.

Obviously the birds were commanding us to leave: *warning, warning, warning*. Their instruction was direct, simple: *Scram!* It struck over and over, sounding like some ancient music, a music so intense it plays not around you but into you until finally you surrender to a performance you don't necessarily watch as much as you eerily feel.

On that windy, urban cliff in Manhattan I imagined the peregrine and the human two million years ago, the beginning of both species, when the peregrine lived amidst *Homo habilis*—the "handy man" who made tools, walked upright, and who could speak. Over the centuries, the peregrine and *Homo habilis*, and then the later fire-maker, *Homo erectus,* and the modern *Homo sapiens*—all of them coexisted as powerful predators alert to each other's presence in the world. Imagine them if you will, scrutinizing their landscapes, calling into stillness, wandering through remoteness, choosing their next kill.

While the MetLife peregrines continued circling, playing their music, I wondered: Is it by sheer chance, some impromptu meeting, that we feel we know a wild creature? Is it that simple, sudden? Or does it rise from something deep and abiding, from a mesmeric relationship developed over centuries perhaps, from experiences buried in the body and triggered now by an angle of light on a wing, by an animal's subtle movement, by its calls and colors, by its beauty, through its death? Maybe the best we can hope for is the belief that we are born prepared for the world, that it is long-settled in us, and that our job is to be hungry for it, to have predatory cravings for it, to stalk it ecstatically, to discover how we know what we know.

By the following summer, a construction site for a new building in the New York Presbyterian Hospital complex was teeming with activity. Contractors argued with engineers, construction workers drilled holes into the earth, hammers pounded, tractors moved masses of urban gray rubble. Ambulances hollered by. I had looked for the hospital peregrines in the autumn over the East River. I had thought about the MetLife pair as my taxi sped down Park Avenue, but I'd not seen or heard the birds since the banding of the MetLife nestlings.

Stationed and ready to spend the day by the hospital construction site, I hoped to glimpse the new brood of peregrine fledglings, who at this time in their young lives would be practicing their flying and, with their parents, would be occupied in hunting lessons. But again they eluded me.

A few days later, walking east on Seventy-second Street, I heard a bird call overhead. Once, and then again, louder: *kek, kek, kek, kek!* I knew it—*peregrine!*—and I looked up. Two falcons skimmed over the fancy Upper East Side brownstones, over the well-dressed workers, the delivery people, the leashed dogs. The parent peregrine handed off prey to its fledgling—one of the ways a young peregrine learns to hunt. They tangled in the air, separated, swooped in circles, called, and flew behind a glass skyscraper toward the East River.

The air filled again with horns, boom boxes, buses, trucks. Like a gift I'd carried around without knowing it, the voice of the falcon had survived in me. The call of the peregrine is no memento, nothing like a feather that can be held in one's hand or stored in a box. It is an heirloom we hold in our bodies, summoning the ghosts within us: our wild past among peregrines.

For All the Girls Who Couldn't Walk into the Woods

I do not fear it: I have been there.
Sylvia Plath

We have cause to feel deeply.
Susan Griffin

There was a woman who lived alone in the woods in a wooden house with many large windows and no curtains. But this woman's tale cannot be told until the stories of older woods—those of the branches, thickets, soils, and creeks that tangle through me like my own blood—are in some small way recalled. And so it will be best to start nearer the end, in the Galápagos Islands of all places, where, however dangerously, I strode through shallow waters of white-tipped reef sharks on my way to a cave at the edge of the sea. From the entrance of the cave I could see more closely the male Galápagos sea lions patrolling the watery lines of their ocean territories during the season of their females—harems of female sea lions on the blood-blotted beach, mothers engaged in birthing or nursing, mothers protecting their pups from roaming male sea lions. Adult males who, when one crossed the blue boundary of another, collided their massive, brown seven-hundred-pound bodies into frothy wars of biting and snorting until the water or beach was pockmarked with blood. I seem always to remember blood.

Such was the case of the male sea lion lounging during the late orange sun of the day, on a different island. My sudden presence near the shadows of the sea lion startled it and it rose, waiting a few minutes to get a bearing and to stare at the breaking waves, before heading toward the green and turbulent sea. Crossing the water-line, relentless and chaotic waves crashed over the sea lion, throwing it onto the hard edges of ancient black stone. When it regained its footing, another sea lion slid up out of dark and churning waters and, in what appeared to be a challenge for the rock, the animals bit and spat, fell, twisted, barked. They kept wrestling, these two sea lions, as the sun began setting beyond their blood-stained necks; and I walked away feeling that this sleepy, besieged sea lion and I now had something in common: We both knew that there is only one way to wake up—immediately aware of the world, fighting for your life as if it mattered.

Truth is, this sort of sea lion life had been, for years and years, mine. Prior to traveling foreign lands, and even before I would come to the woods of the woman's house with many windows, I had traveled through a landscape of my own frothy wars in the place I'd grown up: the suburbs of Washington, D.C., where the clash between predators and between predator and prey first became familiar. Of course it was not supposed to be this way. And looking in from the outside, it was, most likely, an invisible conflict. Should you ask anyone I knew back then to recount the events I am talking about they would say that "boys will be boys," a phrase which forgives, or at the very least denies, the occurrence of assault. But to be accurate, I will have to condense a long stretch of childhood and go to the time of the old woods, to the time my brother was young and a dog was killed.

If it was a dog. Some of the parents said, *fox, of course a fox, who would kill a dog?* as they stood there, coffee mugs in hand on a weekend morning, staring at the burned body of an animal that, they believed, had to have been caught by a gang of boys traveling in the night through the woods that edged our suburban neighborhood. As they spoke I pictured the dog, or fox, running. Some prior injury, I imagined, had made the animal vulnerable. I doubt *vulnera-*

ble was in my vocabulary when I was ten years old; but the feeling of being insufficiently strong, of being unable to run, of being prey —all that was within the realm of everyday life back then, when I had made promises I was determined to keep.

48 ⟨ The promises were for my brother—that I would be there to protect and defend him. Four years older than me and learning disabled, he wore thick glasses and did not play sports. Quiet, sensitive, interested in all things electrical, that was my brother. He could fix your radio that had been full of static for months or hook up all the fancy new video machinery that was invented in his lifetime—switch it from this set to that and make copies at the same time. He ate peanut butter, watched *The Three Stooges* and *The Little Rascals.* The snake he called Houdini rode inside the handlebars of his bicycle on the few occasions he felt brave enough to ride. Swimming pools and snow—he wasn't fond of either, though with the first snowfall of each year he shoveled the driveway, enjoying his accomplishment. But my brother was different. He did not attend the same school as other boys close to his age on our block. Something about him—the learning disability, the glasses, the quiet ways?—made him an object of derision, and he became prey for the pack of neighborhood boys.

I will never know if these were the same boys who killed the fox, or dog. In fact, my parents have no memory of an animal being burned and killed near the woods. They say I awoke often with nightmares and believe that this burned creature appeared in them. Though I think parenthood necessitates bartering one's memories, exchanging the hard times for the easy, the joy over the hurt; otherwise the job can be too defeating. My parents would not deny, however, that there were boys who circled my brother as lions close in on fast-footed ungulates, and took turns beating him on the occasions he ventured into the woods or down to the creek he loved, where he dug up worms for Houdini. I knew because I tagged along behind him, while he yelled back to me, *Go home.* Following my brother and observing the attacks against him became my earliest experiences of tracking, tracking what were, in essence, wild creatures: boys that, in my eyes, were nearly young men.

It did not take long to become wild myself, to know, as prey know, where it is safe and where perhaps it is not. Birds fleeing trees meant the boys were nearby. Slowly, I excelled in discerning the human shape through leaf cover and mastered walking unobtrusively, like deer. A squirrel screaming the way it does, like a needle scratching over a record, was a cue of something amiss. Identifying the territories of boys, their carports, yards, or the stretch of creek where they often lurked, or which vine in the woods they would be hanging on during a particular time of the day or year—all of this became second nature. Probably before it was necessary for a young girl to know it so viscerally, I learned to read the body's expressions of power: a stare of the eyes, a clench of the jaw and tightening of the lips, a particular swagger, a well-timed laugh, a verbal insult, a smile, even, or all-out rage. I soaked up this knowledge as a plant soaks up water, while I watched the boys struggle to determine who would be the dominant male in the pack to deliver—in the secretive vines and trees of the woods—the first bloody blow to my brother, the best bite.

Years later, to get to the woman's wooden house in the woods, it was necessary to drive the winding roads of rural, upstate New York. Along these roads it is common to pass more than a few dented trailer homes with windows curtained in bedsheets and, in the yards, incessantly barking and muddy dogs leashed to chains. The woman's house was an anomaly in these parts. It was not painted—not mint green or pink or royal blue—and was, in fact, so plain it easily could be mistaken for a stand of trees, if you even noticed it. With help from a few friends, this woman built her home in the early seventies. But as soon as I met her, I figured her to be the type to create a house in dark woods in the middle of nowhere. She was an artist, a dancer who chose the road less traveled, along the way discarding a television in favor of NPR, and holding on

for all the girls...

to her Joni Mitchell, Crosby, Stills & Nash, and Grateful Dead al-
bums, as well as her photos of Woodstock, which she attended
when she was in her forties, and bared her chest.

When we met, she was sixty, and even with her older body and
gray hair she was still the epitome of the aging, freewheeling hip-
pie, tempered a bit by the fact that she was, and had been for quite
some time, a college dance professor at a prestigious school, traveling often with her dance troupe, which is why I came to know her.
Her cat needed looking after, as did her wooden house with many
windows and no curtains. Even the large bathroom, on the ground
floor, was a room of doors and glass panes.

"What do you need curtains for?" I remember her asking after I
questioned the openness of her home. "You have the woods, trees,
what else could you need? Come back," she had said, "spend time
here, with the cat, before I leave."

And so I did, during daylight, when she made fresh bread,
which we slathered with butter before we ate the apple crisp she'd
made from apples that somehow managed to grow in the shady soil
of her land.

I arrived for my two-week cat-sitting job, on the sunny morning she was to leave, to a kitchen with a piping hot pan of yet more
apple crisp and, also, to a well-stocked fridge, because the grocery
was so far away, she explained, like everything else. She seemed
happy—as she packed the last of her things and the cat jumped
up and down from the counter—that at least I'd have food. Maybe
this would be rosy, I thought, smelling the apple crisp while attempting to keep on my lap the cat who had the run of the place,
entering and exiting through an unlocked and perpetually swinging front door.

"Oh, that door, I don't lock it. The cat...," the woman trailed
off, picking up her luggage to carry to the door. "And here's a sign
you will need if you go out. Please put it on the front door."

"A sign for what?"

She explained that twice recently, and three times if you

counted the last, which didn't really count, men had broken into her home and had robbed her of her food. "Just my food," she said, "nothing else."

"Men . . . ?"

"Well, they didn't break the door. Like I said, I don't lock it. Just that I came home and the food in the fridge was scattered across the counter. Some they ate, they left the butter, they took the vegetables, the meat, the bread. It was a mess. That's what really burned me up. The mess. I put up the sign after the second break-in," she said, trying to clarify things. "It asks them to please clean up after themselves. The third time they came, they cleaned up!"

Against my instincts, I chose not to abandon this woman. I was young when this happened and had, however misguided, the invincibility of a college student off on my own for the summer in the countryside of Ithaca, New York. Though to be honest the deciding factor was more practical than sympathetic: between apartments, I had no place to stay.

At night, alone in her house without curtains, I turned off the lights, turned on NPR, and sat on the couch, with the intention of permanently residing there until daylight. Outside, it was pitch black. Without a street, there were no street lamps, no neighbors, no porch lamps. If there were men out there, it seemed wise to remain unseen behind the huge glass windows. Over the next two weeks I tossed and turned the nights in blackness. I locked the doors; NPR sang me to sleep. During the day, I retreated to the woods, convinced that, paradoxically, the forest offered the quickest route of escape. The men might come out of the trees, but I went in, nonetheless. On the old, wide-trunked trees curious red efts stopped to stare at me; the shades of their brilliant orange and red bodies seeming, to me, to subtly change shade when I talked to them. Sometimes I followed the woman's cat through the woods while she hunted. We searched for the flutist melodies of wood thrush and heard deer crash through the bush.

But then, I had been in woods before.

for all the girls . . .

I had thought about boys and men and woods before.

And I was reminded—as I sat against a tree trunk reading books about women and nature—that, once, long ago, I had been a different person, before I knew neighborhood boys, before I knew men.

There was a time I walked without fear. I suspect many girls did, in the early years of a girl's life, when we do not think of our bodies in the ways we will come to think of them later, as women. We possessed, simply, bodies of childhood, ebullient, sparkling. And for each of us the landscape of youth was still an animistic landscape, wherein the creatures, plants, rocks, and rivers dwelling outside had the potential to dwell—intimately, sensually, symbiotically—inside our young minds and muscles.

When I was in elementary school, my father's job transferred him from our home in the Washington, D.C., suburbs to Winchester, Massachusetts, where we rented a house near the rim of an abandoned gravel pit that was in the process of becoming a strong forest once again. Along the west and south rim, grasses grew so long and full that they fell over, forming soft green moguls in the heat and brittle, bisque-colored bumps in the cold. The walls of the pit below the moguls balanced rocks, seedlings, and wildflowers. On the north and east rims were patches of forest that had once covered the entire area, and from the north flowed a trembling and skinny creek that long ago, when it was wider and stronger, must have ruled the land. Now, when the water reached the edge of the pit it spilled down weakly—a waterfall in my eyes—and became a pond in the belly of the beast, where bushes tangled over one another and saplings reached through the gravel and sand that the road crews had left behind.

The pit and the forest. I went to them every day, often with my brother, who was still lively—like a bear cub—rambunctious, curious, free-running. We met black racers and box turtles; butterflies, blue jays, robins; and green and purple dragonflies that we believed would sew shut our mouths if we didn't quiet ourselves as they flew by. We fell through thin ice, lollygagged in sunshine. We imagined: There was a troll who guarded the cave near the pond, and we rode camels in the sand. The pit. Kid culture. Wildness.

In New York City, where I went to live after Ithaca, I was pulled toward anything that "spoke pit"—trees, birds, rocks, water. I moved to the small, unnoticed lives around me. On my fire escape I grew millet in a ceramic planter to attract house finches that brought their babies by. On my way out each day, I touched the leaves of the white ash growing in front of my building. Its roots reached below the street and into soil that once was home to Jones Woods, a 160-acre forest that in the mid-1800s ran from the East River to Third Avenue between Sixty-sixth and Seventy-fifth streets.

New York was not my pit. But I was not in Winchester, and nature is not always somewhere besides where I am. I took what I could get.

I remember the hot summer day my husband and I rode the A train to Inwood Hill, a 196-acre forest and salt marsh oasis on the northwestern tip of the city. Zipping underground like a mole through the dark tunnels of Manhattan, I envisioned this land, my home, just over three centuries ago: completely forested, ringed with tidal marshes, walked upon by the last Native Americans— members of the Algonquin Nation—to live there before being swindled out of the island by Europeans. I was heading for the remnants of that land, knowing I'd be lucky to see the one muskrat a friend told me built a lodge in the saltwater cordgrass of Inwood's marsh. On the train, my husband talked about the glacier that covered Manhattan fifteen thousand years ago with a wall of ice more than two thousand feet high. At Inwood there are boulders the ice left behind. He imagined Inwood marble, the rock below the Manhattan schist where the skyscrapers he designs are anchored.

Mostly, though, I thought about the beauty of the woods— maples, tulip trees, oaks, black cherries, birches, ferns, wildflowers, songbirds, insects; light ribboned around leaves.

We arrived at Inwood. In the marsh one great egret, looking

for all the girls...

like a flame of white fire in the water, skewered an invertebrate with its bill. The muskrat? Could have been—certainly there was an entrance to a dwelling in the cordgrass. Twelve mallards, four Canada geese, and two snowy egrets lingered by the pond. We heard an oriole and looked for it in a London plane planted near the marsh, which is fenced in to protect it from park visitors chasing misdirected footballs. At the southwest tip of the marsh we took a left and walked south through the manicured lawns where fathers wrestled with sons and a mother tied pink birthday balloons to a tree.

The woods: we entered. Tall trees, lush, unkempt, and unparklike, darkened the path, which was a dying human artifact stabbed by weeds, moss, grass. The soil was cooled chocolate; the air was breezy. Here, away from the sounds of the city, I could hear the leaves of trees, scratching, swaying; it was the small patch of paradise I envisioned until I heard the voice: *Don't go into the woods. . . .* It was the voice of my mother, protecting me from the older boys who harassed, humiliated, and beat my brother. And it soon became my voice, the one calling to my brother, attempting to stop him from entering the scene of his own demise. It is still the voice that plucks me out of the place I want to be most, as though the land is somehow as culpable as the thugs inhabiting it. In all actuality it is any maternal voice—even the voice of the Galápagos sea lion mother—calling her children away from danger, toward safety. It is a voice similar to that spoken on my college campus, which required female students returning to dorms from the library after nightfall to use the escort service provided by the other men— those who protect us. The harmless men? The harmful men? When all women want is to walk onward, by ourselves.

It is hard to pinpoint, exactly, when a girl comes to understand what for men is the seemingly ancient knowledge "that [their] genitalia [can] serve as a weapon to generate fear," which "must rank as one of the most important discoveries of prehistoric times, along with the use of fire and the first crude stone axe," says feminist writer Susan Brownmiller.

Even with a man, a woman is not necessarily safe. Women are

usually raped by men they know; and though we have husbands, brothers, fathers, and male friends, their presence does not guard against other men. Women know this.

One out of four women in the United States will be raped. Though of course thoughts of rape do not penetrate every moment, the fear can be strong in a woman's life, in my life, no matter where I am, whom I'm with. "Wherever you go you are warned of danger outside or from beyond some perimeter," said writer Mary Catherine Bateson, the daughter of world travelers and intellectuals Margaret Mead and Gregory Bateson. Warning stories are all around. The woman in New Jersey a few years ago who was riding her bike in the country when suddenly she was knocked down and pulled into the woods by a man who tortured and raped her. Along the road leading to my university, a woman was dragged into the woods by two men who raped her repeatedly before burning her to death. There is a friend's sister—raped and left in the woods near a creek, mouth taped, feet and hands bound. There are the two women who, hiking the Appalachian Trail a few years ago, still have not been found. I think of my own brushes. After a day of hiking along the Appalachian Trail with a friend, and while pounding stakes into the earth for our tent, a man broke through the lovely green walls of the forest, in the late afternoon when the sun was dark pink, nearly crimson. He swaggered up to me, waved his bloody hunting knife across the air of my face, smiled, and reported that he had just butchered a deer. Then he left, as silently as he had come.

And I cannot forget the evening after a day spent with trees and an esteemed, married, and older biologist to whose college campus I had traveled by bus from Manhattan. We'd had a long and appropriately professional time in the field, talking of Canada geese, woodchucks, falcons, sunrays, animal communication. During dinner at a small Italian place by the bus depot, where I was waiting for my bus ride home, and to where the biologist had invited himself, I took an aspirin.

"I guess that's your way of telling me you're not going to bed with me tonight," he said, staring straight into my eyes with a slight smile, and, after sipping his red wine, a tiny well-timed laugh—the body's expressions of power I had learned long ago, from the seasons my brother was sacrificed.

I left.

It is second nature for me to be alert to non-point-source sounds —footsteps, whistles; to be aware of shadows, movement; to have keys in hand long before arriving at the car door, the house door. It's a necessary instinct.

My husband, of course, does not have this instinct. Nor did the dancer with the wooden house and many windows. Clearly some— perhaps many—women do not. But there are others like me, other girls who couldn't walk into the woods—not because they didn't want to but because in Northeastern forests the biggest threat may be the male *Homo sapiens*.

The additional details about my brother's blood-stained clothing, crying or trying not to, his black eyes, bruised body, and swollen nose—all of this can be imagined. I remember wishing only that my brother had a brother, an ally, instead of me. Through the years, while he fought, or even surrendered, I crouched beside the old box turtle or stroked the soft mockingbird feather across my forehead. It seems that now, in retrospect, there is something to be learned from the lives of crows, who forage in garbage and are strengthened by roadkill. They grow from eating what is typically thought of as ugly in much the same way I grew to know the forest through that which was violent and cruel. While tracking my brother and his assailants, while attempting and failing to help him, while waiting and watching him fall, there were, always, other lives in the woods. "The greatest delight which the fields and woods minister," wrote Emerson, "is the suggestion of an occult relation between [human and nonhuman]. I am not alone and unacknowledged. They nod to me, and I to them." In the woods of my brother's persecution, strong-voiced crows called, as though companions of ours; snakes by the creek and skinks the color of rainbows; deer walking in wild

the hopes of snakes

berries; patient, quiet turtles—comrades all, fellow warriors engaged in their own struggles. Deer versus hunter; turtle versus moving car; snake versus society. The experience of dread and beauty, I learned in the woods of childhood, can be simultaneous.

Those warm summer days at the dancer's house, during which the men never appeared, were proof of what philosopher Norman O. Brown once wrote: "What is always speaking silently is the body." A woman's musical body, yearning for the song of wood thrush; a woman's daring body, running not from but toward the crash of deer in bush; a woman's gentle body, conversing with salamanders; a woman's curious body, following the adventures of a cat. A woman's body as strong as a sea lion, a body that senses there is only one way to wake up: immediately aware of the world, fighting for your life not as if it mattered but because it matters.

Violence undermines trust—not just in men but in the world. The natural course of things is that girls grow up. We walk through shallow waters of sharks because already we have walked with boys, and, later, with men. We feel empathy for sea lion mothers because we know what it is to protect what we love: our brothers, sisters, men, women, or the land: the woods unknown by those who have never been in them, by those who would burn them, log them, build in them.

"Our task," wrote Rilke, "is to stamp this provisional, perishing earth into ourselves so deeply, so painfully and passionately, that its being may rise again, invisibly, in us." Women must walk, then, with prowess and with company, into the woods, into our own wildness, into the tangled forest of what it is to be female.

for all the girls...

Rediscovering the Potomac

I am rocking in a sixty-foot-long boat on the Potomac River, under a massive concrete arch of the Francis Scott Key Bridge that connects Virginia to Washington, D.C. It is a late summer morning, and although I know another workday in Washington is heating up —the coffee shop doors are squeaking open and road-raged commuters are honking their horns—the most I hear from my spot on the river is the resonant humming of the 7:00 A.M. traffic racing across the six lanes above me. It's river time on the water, a time of day that has played itself out for eons. It's when the barred owls have departed the matte gray sky and the herons have arrived to fish; when the sycamores patiently reach for the new day's burgeoning light, morning after morning after morning.

While I wait with seven people—my crew—for our rowing coach to begin a race between our boat and another, I dip my hand into the river that surrounds, almost swallows, our skinny boat. The green satin current splits around my fingers as I stretch them straight. Quickly, though, I pull my hand out. The water stings the blisters the other rowers and I show off almost as badges of honor, resulting from the friction of river, oar, and skin. But deep down I feel, too, that the river has been searing its way into me since before the rowing season began this past spring. Blisters reveal only one, physical, point of entry. There have been others.

Three-and-a-half miles northwest of where we wait below Key Bridge is a rocky span of the river called Little Falls, where I live in Maryland. When I watch the Potomac outside the window of my study, I watch a river that has meandered east and south from its headwaters in West Virginia. By the time it reaches my house, already it has traveled some 270 of its 383 miles.

59

Little Falls is a place of some significance, since it is here that the Potomac turns into a tidal estuary just as it enters the city of Washington. Some eighty-four species of fish, such as herring, striped bass, and sturgeon, use the forty-mile span of the river from Little Falls through the city and beyond as a spawning and nursery area. And some four million people live within the river's Washington-area watershed. In George Washington's day, the largest ships of the ocean navigated up the Potomac to what is now Georgetown—the oldest section of the city with its steep, cobble-stoned streets—delivering cargo to this frontier land. In Washington's mind, the riverfront would expand into a place of fabulous markets and exchanges; it would be a place where he envisioned a great city. His city. My city. The country's city: Washington, D.C.

East of Key Bridge and into the heart of the city is the boat-house from where we launched. Across the river from the boathouse is an eighty-eight-acre leafy green island memorial for our twenty-sixth president, Theodore Roosevelt, a conservationist who during one of his speeches roared: "I hate a man who would skin the land." Blanketed with forests, Roosevelt Island is a haven for beaver, red-tailed hawk, great horned owl, opossum, and the occasional fox. I imagine it's the sort of refuge President Nixon must have dreamed of escaping to when, just across the river, behind the glass-and-concrete convolutions of the infamous Watergate building, his misdeeds were unearthed.

Beyond Watergate, for the next eight or so miles south, the river runs through a picture-perfect postcard of the nation's capital—snaking alongside the Kennedy Center, the Lincoln Memorial, the FDR Memorial, the Jefferson Memorial, the Pentagon, and Reagan National Airport toward the southern tip of the city near the

Woodrow Wilson Bridge. Some one hundred miles beyond the Wilson Bridge the Potomac melts into the Chesapeake Bay.

The city's sites quickly pass our river-splashed eyes. It is only when we paddle slowly or stop that there's time to acknowledge where I am along the Potomac. Idle chitchat is not allowed on the boat. The bunch of us who row at 5:45 A.M. appear from the dim corridors of the metro area, greet one another, row until 7:45 A.M., and leave. That I have recently returned to the Washington area after living in Manhattan for nearly fifteen years; that my young daughter waits for me at home; that if the person in front of me would look up to the sky she would see the six-foot wingspan of a great blue heron flying over the boat, and how glorious is that!?— all of this I cannot say. As much as rowing is a team sport, it is also a necessarily solitary one; the strongest relationship I nurture is the one with the river and its landscape.

It was about this time last summer when my husband, my then nearly three-year-old daughter Madeleine, and I came to live in an old neighborhood on a ridge along the Potomac. Our small stone cottage is so close to the city limits of Washington that if I climbed the fifty-foot oak across the street, I would likely see the top of the Washington Monument.

That first day we arrived, the weather was typical for a summer day in Washington—sweltering, oppressive, with a thunderstorm threatening to roll in. My body instantly registered the heat as something familiar from my childhood spent in the Washington suburbs of the Potomac River watershed. Thunderstorms, a neighbor informed me—in that helpful way new neighbors have of telling you everything they know about your new home, perceiving your lack of experience with the place—run up the Potomac like tornadoes, ripping through the floodplain forest of sycamore, beech, oak, red maple, and elm. You'll need to buckle down, the neighbor said, stay inside.

So we headed out. My daughter dashed ahead of me, like a fledgling, into her new land. We walked toward the floodplain forest that is protected within the C&O Canal National Historic Park. Thunderclouds passed as we made our way over a lock on the canal and through the underbrush, drawn by the sound of the river crashing around rocks. Though, as I walked, I thought my neighbor's perception of me might be right. I had lived in Washington long ago; after such an absence, perhaps I *was* like a greenhorn in a new country.

Twelve hours earlier, just that morning, I had parted with a landscape to which I was deeply attached, a small forested parcel of parkland near my apartment along New York City's East River. The East River, with her roily currents, slow sighs, colors, and creatures restored some peace into the hectic lifestyle that is Manhattan. My daughter took her very first steps outdoors in those trees by the East River. And although there was no green shoreline to the water, penned in as it was by seawalls and a city highway, my girl and I walked along the iron-and-concrete promenade every day. It was the most urbanized body of water I'd ever known, yet it managed to nourish the lives of the peregrine falcons, cormorants, fish, snapping turtles, and herons that made their homes along it.

It was difficult to leave the East River behind. But as my daughter grew I began to understand her birth as an invitation for my husband and me to leave New York. Living as hard-core urbanites for so long, we fantasized about relocating to some cabin in the backcountry of Minnesota. We considered the northern California coast. But our thoughts turned again and again to the river that had raised us and the landscape that had nurtured us: the Potomac River watershed.

Back in Washington and traversing the promenade of the Potomac all these years later, I felt the land of my childhood reinhabiting me: The smell of wet soil and rotting logs, the scraping sound of long wild grass against my legs and the asthmatic squealing *keeer-r-r* of a red-tailed hawk, a flash of a pileated woodpecker's flaming red crest high in the green trees. I was overcome with feeling strangely lost yet found at the same time. I imagined it must be what a migrating bird experiences: a sudden departure from one

rediscovering the potomac

terrain and arrival in another. In the new-old land, the bird begins a quest of belonging again, an adventure in re-placing itself.

I scooped my daughter up and watched her survey the river. Her eyes followed a belted kingfisher rattling down the shoreline, heading for the city.

"This is *Wash-ing-ton*," I said.

"Big sky," Madeleine answered, clearly dazzled.

She was beginning to speak for the world. And she was right. Compared to the enormous verticality of the Manhattan skyline she was used to, with its eclectic mix of skyscrapers, Washington's skyline was barely one at all, almost horizontal in its low-lying expansiveness.

As we headed home, she dabbled in the dusk, charmed with the magnificence of simple things along the path: ladybugs, wild pink roses, potato bugs, and buttercups. Like the saplings surrounding her willowy body, she stood in front of me, a gift to the land. I envisioned her ripening over the years with the young trees, harboring the stories of the Potomac, growing into the landscape she would call her own.

Paddling the boat upriver one day in spring, the coach yelled, "Beaver!" Everyone on the boat was anxious to see a beaver since, several weeks before, three beavers had captured the city's attention by chopping down several trees from the renowned cherry tree grove near the Tidal Basin, a peaceful, pondlike body of water that opens into the Potomac River.

It was a sensitive area the beavers attempted to infiltrate, an area that attracts tourists eager to stroll around the white marble splendor of the Jefferson and Lincoln memorials and the fastidiously groomed green parkland. I'll admit I was disappointed when a trapper caught and relocated the city's comical fugitives. The animals had shown Washingtonians that as much as the city is an urban landscape, it also harbors, through the lure of the Potomac, a wild landscape.

Back on the boat, in the second it took me to turn to see the coach's beaver, it had disappeared. The rest of the crew missed it as well, and there was a collective sigh of disappointment.

I've come upon a beaver once, with my husband and daughter as we rode our bikes into the city along the C&O Canal's towpath. I swerved to miss the suddenly evident scaly paddle of a tail. Immediately, we stopped. The beaver slid down the bank of the canal and into the water. Hoping it might resurface in the cool morning we were sharing, we waited.

A fervor ran through me, an excitement in knowing that the woods and the stream were the beaver's world. I think often there is the tendency to believe that the landscape of the city and the suburbs is a rather empty one, to believe that nature exists more fully in the countryside. Indeed, the preservation of open, undeveloped space is essential, critical to wildlife. But I feel the need to appreciate, also, the beaver living on the city line, the urban beaver that is both a gift from the wilder world as well as a reminder that in some ways we have failed that wilder place. My near collision with the beaver was one of those capricious moments that makes irreclaimable the mundane routine of life before that instant. It was like a dream that splits open your mind, revealing to you your hidden happiness or loves. And from then on, whenever you recall the dream, you feel the tiniest bit different in the world.

Soon after the encounter with the towpath beaver, I took Madeleine to a stream that feeds into Cabin John Creek, a tributary of the Potomac near our home, to search for beavers I'd read were living there. We drove along a bustling suburban road busy with the latest SUVs and an assortment of service vans and trucks. Just off the roadside we found the spot: a mangled little valley of some forty downed trees situated in a neighborhood of expensive homes hidden in the woods.

I carried Madeleine through the green underbrush and toward the water. We walked near some maples the beavers had left like pencil points precariously balanced against one another in the stark sunlit morning and slid our fingers over the waves of teeth marks the animals had sculpted into the wood. Madeleine stuffed her pockets with the beavers' scattered wood chips, for later examination, for when, she said, "I will play beaver."

At the bank of the stream we followed a slide of grass down to the muddy, pebbly shoreline. Madeleine, expecting a rush of beavers in the sunshine, spotted a bulky and well-camouflaged American toad hiding behind a broad old leaf. Its black eyes seemed to sink into the orbits of its skull as we bent down closer. Which is when I saw that the toad was injured; two large patches of abraded skin revealed the pink muscle of its stout and solid body.

Because it did not move, Madeleine believed it was waiting for her to hold it. I showed her the animal's wounds and explained that lifting the toad might hurt it. What had happened, she wanted to know? I could only guess. A deer's hoof scraped it? A car's wheel sideswiped it? A fox pinned it to the ground, though somehow it escaped?

"Let's leave it here," I whispered.

In the typical battle of wills that her age brings, she insisted that the toad was waiting for her. She was certain the animal was in need of her and, by extension, that the earth was in need of her help. Caught between wishing to encourage my daughter's compassion and wanting to let the toad die peacefully, I tried, "Let's let the toad rest while we get more chips to take home to play beaver."

But in her mind this time was much like several others. And she recalled them: Stopping on the way to the grocery store for an injured robin in the street; snatching the brown snake out from under the rake; escorting the box turtle across a suburban boulevard on a rainy day; relocating the praying mantis off the driveway. She was correct on all counts, and I was humbled by the detailed memories children carry within them.

"Is it going to die?" she asked without looking at me.

"Probably," I said, sensing that because she knew death already —through the loss of her cat—I could tell her what I believed to be true about the dire-looking toad.

"But . . . ," she trailed off.

"But what?"

"The leaf will cover the toad. It will be safe. And the beaver will be here."

"Well," I paused, "maybe the toad will grow new skin."

"Well," she paused, copying and interrupting me at the same time, "maybe the leaf will cover the toad and the beaver will take care of it."

There was no point in telling her otherwise.

It is said that children are our teachers, like little Buddhas placed in our path. In their own way, they have a vivid understanding that a community other than a human one lives around them. I suppose my daughter imbued this community with compassion because she listened to the thoughts of her heart. And although rationality, biology, everything proven, told me a leaf and a beaver wouldn't rescue the toad, I left the stream singed by her idea of a sentient landscape.

Sometimes while on the boat I long to point out to my crewmates that a fish just shot out of the water, or that the black serpentine neck floating nearby is not a miniature Loch Ness monster but that of the double-crested cormorant.

But I mostly wish that a bald eagle, our national symbol, would soar over the boat and thrill us. A pair of eagles has recently taken up residence within the city limits, an event that, having last occurred fifty-three years ago, speaks to the improving quality of the Potomac and its fishery. Because these eagles are what biologists call first-year nesters—something like being a nervous newlywed and a new parent at the same time—the location of the nest remains undisclosed until the birds fully establish themselves.

The nests of Washington's other two pairs of bald eagles are situated like bookends to the metropolitan area. In only the last three years, a pair has settled in a cove on the Maryland shore of the Potomac, just over the city limits at the southeastern boundary of Washington, a scant half mile from the heavily trafficked Woodrow Wilson Bridge. From their cove, the eagles soar on seven-foot wingspans to forage over the Potomac, silhouetting themselves against the distant backdrop of the city.

In a more serene setting ten miles northwest of the city, at a place on the river called Great Falls, lives another pair of eagles. At Great Falls the Potomac explodes through a rock-and-boulder-strewn, almost prehistoric, landscape as it descends seventy-six feet in a dramatic series of falls. The eagles' nest is above the falls, as a park ranger explained it, in a giant sycamore tree leaning into the river's green water. "You can't miss it," he said cheerily.

When I was a kid in the 1970s, Great Falls was my refuge—a place to hike flowered trails, swing on vines like Tarzan through the trees, climb gray cliffs, navigate shallow streams of the river. Thanks to the toxic effects of the pesticide DDT, though, it was not a refuge for eagles. Back then, fewer than five hundred nesting pairs of eagles remained in the lower forty-eight states. Now, five hundred nesting pairs live in Maryland and Virginia alone, while several hundred immature, or nonbreeding, nomadic eagles roost in the winter along secluded areas of the Potomac. Some of those nomads—twelve have been counted—use six miles of the Potomac within Washington to feast on the exposed fish at low tide.

It was a nomadic, immature eagle that landed during a long, slow rain one day in the fifty-foot oak tree across from my house, where it, too, might have seen the Washington Monument had the river valley not been fogged over. An intensity flames through you when you see a wild eagle for the first time. It's as though, as the mystic Rumi said, "We are alive with other life." You feel more clearly the slope of the tree the eagle is in, the texture of the land you're standing on, the smell of the sky, the color of the wind.

All of this, while the eagle sat hunkered down like a general on the front line, inciting crows into black arrows of rage and desperation. The eagle may be the god of birds to us, but it was Lucifer to the crows: They demanded their tree back. For twenty minutes the eagle perched on the oak, which was forever to me, before weaving its brown wings into a cape to grab the fog and go.

Somehow, I never saw the eagles at Great Falls, though I did spot their grand nest in the sycamore. Perhaps seeing the eagles was less important than knowing they are thriving along the Potomac. Even when there is no encounter, there is still the kindling of anticipation, the private thoughts of huge brown wings hunting over you.

Rowing downstream one spring morning, we quietly passed herons fishing off the shore of Roosevelt Island. Without stopping, we rowed along the Washington shoreline of Rock Creek Park, passing the mouth of Rock Creek that opens into the Potomac. I tried to get a good look at these spots along the river because one of them held the answer to a certain mystery: the mystery of two red foxes, a male and female, that somehow came to live on a golf course in downtown Washington. Rowing along the river, I tried to imagine the foxes traveling to the golf course in the two ways naturalists theorize it could have happened during a night in 1996.

If the foxes arrived by land, they tumbled out of the 2,100 acres of wooded national parkland that make up Rock Creek Park within the city limits of Washington. Rock Creek itself meanders thirty miles through the Maryland countryside and the suburbs outside the city before cutting through Washington and empty-ing into the Potomac just over a mile from the White House. Great stands of tulip poplars, oak, ash, birch, and hickory blanket the steep hillsides of what are the remains of the city's ancient mountains.

In 1890 Congress described Rock Creek as a place of "pleasant valleys and deep ravines, primeval forests and open fields" and set it aside as the first urban natural area. The deep ravines and dark forests of Rock Creek still exist, though a web of houses, embassies, and offices surrounds them. Some twelve million drivers a year use the park's thoroughfares, and two million people a year hike, bike, and horseback ride in the park. Yet, surprisingly, Rock Creek re-mains a refuge for deer, raccoon, beaver, flying squirrel, great horned owl, red-tailed hawk, Eastern screech owl, dozens of song-birds, a variety of amphibians and reptiles, as well as muskrat, opossum, groundhog, and gray and red fox.

Whispering themselves out of the leafy enclaves of Rock Creek Park would have been, for the foxes, the easy part. They would then have had to travel several dark miles through the city, along high-ways, around government buildings and presidential memorials, and over a small bridge to reach their destination: a drainage ditch flanking a hillock on the golf course. The golf course is the wildest part of Washington's seven-hundred-acre Potomac Park, an urban green space that begins just off the busy city streets and leads down to the Potomac River.

The second itinerary takes us directly to a night on the Po-tomac, during the wrath of hurricane-force winds and flood-level waters. It is possible—picture it if you will—that the river surged into the floodplain forest and grabbed two foxes from the syca-mores. The foxes, not adept swimmers, would have had to float through the black storm on a log, perhaps, the current landing them at the golf course.

Thanks to rowing, it is my habit to wake early, early enough to get to Potomac Park by dawn and glimpse the foxes as they return to their den after a night of foxy duties: stalking rats and mice by the Vietnam Veterans Memorial, scent-marking the woods by the FDR Memorial, caching into sand piles on the golf course any fish that may have washed up along the Potomac.

Over the weeks I've pieced together the foxes' story: When the golf course superintendent spotted the animals in the drainage ditch, he, being a man who enjoys foxes, allowed the hillock to grow over, unkempt and wild. By the following spring, the foxes had kits that frolicked in the grass of the eighteen-hole course that is in such demand that golfers arrive at 6:00 A.M. to be assured a chance to play. Other piles of soil grew over, more foxes were born, now there are nine. Some mornings, the foxes can be seen playfully pouncing on golf balls as they roll by. Yet they've been working, too. Since their arrival, they've eased the park's overpopulated species of squirrel, Canada goose, seagull, and rat.

Arriving at the golf course, I walked toward the summer river, through the tang of fresh-cut grass that smelled like the backyards of suburbia. Crouched down near a scruffy hill, I saw a dart of bright rust-colored fur dash across the smooth grass. Then another. Minutes later, two more. The breeze, though, was betraying me, revealing the scent of my skin and the sounds of my minute movements. The first three foxes bolted into the den. But the fourth sat on its haunches, head cocked in doglike curiosity, watching. I felt the great privilege of being not only recognized and tolerated by a wild animal, but also of being the subject of its interest.

I wondered if seeing the foxes in such a setting might alleviate what seems to be a growing fear of the animals in the area. Recently, more than 430 nuisance calls from my Maryland county were made to wildlife officials about foxes. And a woman I read about in the paper had a fox den near her suburban home exterminated, fearing the vixen and her mate "could eat you up in a gulp."

The poet Kahlil Gibran said in *The Prophet*: "Your soul is oftentimes a battlefield upon which your reason and your judgment wage war against your passion and your appetite." Could the incongruity of foxes coexisting with people on a golf course be a blessing, something that might calm the battle we wage with predators? If, as predicted by the United Nations, an astonishing 80 percent of the population of the United States will live in cities in the year 2010, our urban and suburban landscapes will need to be reenvisioned as the primary places to sustain our passion for the wildlife living among us.

Meanwhile, in front of me a splendid red fox was perched, its plumy, luxuriant tail spilling around its paws. There was a deliciousness in the air, like the great pleasure that floats between two who immediately attract. Eventually, the careful and slow movement of bringing my binoculars to my eyes frightened the fox, and it slid away into the shadows.

I peered toward the city in the background, toward the Washington Monument and the modern office buildings standing like glass mountains reflecting the new day's sunlight. As surreal as it was, the golf course flickered in my mind like a seething Serengeti, where the foxes were the lions and the gulls were the gazelles. I felt reassured by this territory, by the fact that evolution continues to sculpt the minds and bodies of urban predator and prey. Looking around, I saw the park as a microcosm of the larger world of the metropolitan fox, which flames along the Potomac and through the suburbs, quickening the landscape, sustaining it with winners and losers, life and death.

My scattered remembrances of the riverscape fade as my thoughts return to the morning's race from Key Bridge back to the boathouse. Vigorously slicing my oars through the water, I arrive at the dock, soaked from the waist down. I wipe the sweat from my brow and help the crew lift the boat out of the Potomac. Fifteen minutes later I am on my way home.

Driving along the city streets, I plan my day with my daughter. We could walk along the canal and listen for the whistle of a Northern oriole or the flutelike melody of a wood thrush. Maybe we could manage to sneak by a great blue heron patiently fishing in the canal without startling it out of its steadfastness. Or we could head to the place we befuddled the beaver.

I think of greeting Madeleine. In her sleepy state she will tell me, in all seriousness, how she too has just returned from rowing, how she was rowing in my boat, but I did not see her. I delight in how she imagines herself into the Potomac.

In the time we've lived here, she has reimagined the landscape of the Washington area for me as well, sharing the world of a child through her impromptu discernments: "Bees paint the tulips," she exclaimed in the garden one spring day; and "Can you see the melting clouds?" she asked one windy afternoon; and "The sky has glass on it," she described during an ice storm last winter.

In an urban environment—a place in which nature is at times

held in disrepute or ignored—my daughter teaches me that beauty is as much a state of mind as a state of the land.

I turn into my neighborhood, pass neighbors walking their dogs, pull into my driveway, and hurry to let go of the steering wheel that has aggravated my blisters. In the sky, an airplane uses the river as a road and follows it toward Reagan National Airport, while a traffic helicopter zips upriver to the rush-hour chaos on the beltway. It is 8:30, and morning is in full swing. I hear blue jays squabbling and watch squirrels race through the trees. Overhead, a community of crows mobs a red-tailed hawk. The birds pepper the sky with their zest, asserting their convictions and intentions. And I stand fused to this busy land by the river, enjoying the aerial dramas of a new day, feeling acutely that just "to be here," as the poet Rilke wrote, "is so much."

A Banishment of Crows

One for sorrow, two for joy,
Three for a girl, four for a boy,
Five for silver, six for gold,
Seven for a secret ne'er to be told.
Mother Goose

Toward the end of a rainy December day I decide it's a good idea to follow crows flying to their nightly, winter roost—though this will not be accomplished on foot through fields. Tracking crows is best done from one's car, driving through rush hour traffic, with much patience, as well as a bit of honking.

Once, I knew where the crows roosted. In December of 1995, when my daughter Madeleine was an infant, my husband and I brought her to visit our folks for Christmas near Rockville, Maryland, a suburb of Washington, D.C., where we both grew up. One windy day of that vacation we grabbed a video camera and drove to a field where hundreds of crows had gathered to eat corn. I edged toward the birds with my baby sleeping against my chest, hoping that when she awoke the camera would catch the flight of hundreds of crows swirling around her, leaving an early etching of movement, freedom, and mystery on her newborn mind, for it was crows that, in a sense, had been with her since the day she decided to enter the world, in our apartment on the fourth floor of an old red brick house on East Eighty-ninth Street, in New York City.

Immense distractions are necessary during the many hours of labor before birth, when waves of intense and unspeakable pain clearly seem to signal to a first-time mother that her unborn child has, apparently, changed its mind about entering the world: *I'm staying in here!* My distractions were the deeply dark and talkative crows I could see through the slim iron security bars over our open kitchen window. The birds regularly visited the trees and vines in the backyard of the red brick house, where our kitchen was like an inner-city tree fort opening straight into an oasis of green, and into the crows' lives.

It was impossible to know if every day the same group of crows visited, although my husband and I sensed they knew each other well. One preened another. They followed together, hopping and sprinting from branch to branch. One voice answered another. I'd lived in Manhattan nearly ten years by then, and this kitchen window was the first place that the sounds of the city—the annoying car alarms, horns, boom boxes, and endless white noise—didn't drown out the cawing, gurgling, rattling, cooing sounds of crows, birds I didn't know I missed until I heard them again.

As far as I was concerned it was a family of crows that flew in and out of my days that summer, my belly big with my first child. During those hours of labor, I knew the popular symbolism of a crow's appearance: a portent of evil and death, being, as crows are, consumers of carrion. But as they distracted me from my pain, their blackness reminded me of the dark cradle from which my baby was descending.

Black. It is what we see without light to guide us; and within it, whether literally or metaphorically, one inherently seeks light— the light of answers, or questions, even. Is black not the color in which we often choose to make love, and thus is the color of conception? Within utter blackness our brain, skin, bones, heart, our body, forms, and grows. Our eyes first open into it. Life begins in black as black as crows.

A few days after making our video of Madeleine, I stopped at a busy intersection, along Montrose Road, in the city of Rockville, two blocks from the city's main artery, Rockville Pike. It was here, through the car's closed windows, that I heard a persistent and loud

a   b a n i s h m e n t   o f   c r o w s

racket I'd never before heard. Opening the window, I looked out to
what was suddenly a darkening sky. The noise melted over the car.
Flying above me was a river of crows—thousands and thousands of
crows—flowing toward tall and densely packed deciduous trees in
one of the few older wooded areas left in Rockville at the time. Before I'd moved away to New York, I rode by this little forest countless times to drop off, pick up or visit my mother, who worked
for a government health agency nearby. Funny how places in your
hometown become so deeply embedded in you that you no longer
really see them.

The crows continued, flying above Rockville Pike before dropping, by the hundreds, like handfuls of pepper, into the bare
branches of trees along Montrose Road. Their winter chorus grew.
This was their roost, in 1995.

Rockville Pike, or "the Pike" in Maryland vernacular, is an old
road. Stories tell of big historical figures like Benjamin Franklin,
George Washington, Andrew Jackson, James Polk, and troops from
both sides of the Civil War using Rockville Pike as a strategic
travel route during Colonial times. Back then, the Pike wasn't
much more than the dusty Seneca Indian trail it began as, a trail
that started at the mouth of Washington, D.C.'s Rock Creek, a
stream flowing into the Potomac River, and led northwest toward
modern-day Rockville. One historian, Noma Thompson, described,
in her book *Western Gateway to the National Capital: Rockville, Maryland,* the area in the late eighteenth century:

> Large tracts of timberland were cleared for farms and the dense wood-
> land began to thin out due to the building of homes.... Many of the
> Maryland settlers enjoyed lucrative incomes from the crops which
> flourished in a fertile soil and moderate climate. [Yet] within a short
> time after the entrance of the white man into this wildlife sanctu-
> ary... the buffalo, bear and wolf became extinct in the county. At that
> period bounties were paid for wolf scalps. Bobcat and deer, which had
> been plentiful, decreased in numbers.... With the disappearance of
> the old trees and forest boundaries, many birds and wild fowl migrated

to safer havens. . . . In 1800 the farm lands began to deteriorate. . . . The county was regarded as so sterile and unproductive as to be frequently referred to as "the Sahara of Maryland."

Today, agricultural land along the Pike is sparse. The road is, ⟨ 75⟩ rather, one of immense wealth, commercial success and excess, a retailer's religious experience. There are twenty-three shopping centers along just six of the road's forty-two miles, as well as restaurants, apartment buildings, office towers, gas stations, hotels, and car dealers. It is, said a *Washington Post* article in 1997, "one of the East Coast's premier commercial thoroughfares," a place where, "per square foot, retail sales are greater than on [Beverly Hills's] Rodeo Drive." By 2005, ten million more square feet of commercial projects as well as thousands of new homes will have been built. "Those projects will pave over scattered grassy fields and the last farm along the way," reports the *Post*. "When it's all done, there will be few remaining spaces."

It wasn't until 1996 that I discovered development had destroyed most of the crows' roosting site on Montrose Road. Although, as I would later learn, the birds would attempt to return. On my annual Christmas visit home, I drove to see the train of birds tumbling across the sky, coming into Rockville from as far as twenty miles away every evening between October and March. Crows gather in tremendous roosts for the warmth generated by their thousands of bodies stacked together in the winter woods, and for what we might call safety in numbers. The crow's gravest predator is the great horned owl that lives and hunts in woodlands, deserts, even city parks; and it is a silent night stalker, craving the taste of brains and seizing its prey without warning.

Except for a small parcel of trees left at the easternmost corner, one block from the Pike, the crows' roost site had been razed. Old trees sat snapped in half; tractors waited in mire; and a sign advertised: EXCLUSIVE TOWNHOMES TO BE BUILT HERE SOON. Exclusive. Casually, I'd come to associate the word with its secondary definitions: stylish, fashionable, maybe a little snobby. When I was in the magazine publishing business in New York, I asked writers for exclusive rights to their work. Exclusive was special. Looking at the land, I realized how absurdly honest was the sign: the possession of these woods was now limited to humans. Had anyone known about the crow roost, I wondered? Or cared?

"People have strong opinions about crows," said Cornell University professor and crow expert Kevin McGowen, when I went to listen to him lecture at the Smithsonian one night. "Some people are fond of them—the crow's intelligence makes it more human-like than other birds. Most other people, though, generally hate crows."

In his unforgettable words, Edgar Allen Poe described such birds as, "Grim, ungainly, ghastly, gaunt, and ominous." And modern America, it appears, agrees. In the study "Perceptions of Animals in America," Yale professor Stephen Kellert found crows to be one of America's least-liked animals, sharing the title with roaches, rats, rattlesnakes, vultures, and lizards, to name just several. "In much the same way the absence of legs makes the snake unappealing," says McGowan, "the physical appearance of crows—big, black and evil-looking—makes them unpopular."

Unpopular enough to be hunted for the sheer delight of killing. "People shot crows by the hundreds, by the thousands in Buckeystown, north of here," an old Rockville native recalled. "So many crows, the sky black full of them in the seventies. Crow shooters by the hundreds shootin' jus' to get rid of the birds. Probably still do today." Although crows are protected under the migratory bird act, there is a hunting season on them in specified, mostly rural, areas of Maryland.

Down the road from Buckeystown is Darnestown, Maryland, where, I came to find out, an adult female crow had been shot and was discovered dying from the wound. The shot shattered the bird's wing, necessitating an amputation, and now she would live in a three-foot-by-two-foot cage at a nature center while funds could be found to build her a larger outdoor enclosure. "Maybe a teenage boy, a BB gun," mused the naturalist I spoke with when I called to arrange a visit with the crow. Driving to see the bird, I absent-mindedly sang along with an old Earth, Wind & Fire tune on the car radio: "Child is born with a heart of gold / Way of the world, makes his heart grow cold."

Crow. *Corvus brachyrhynchos*. *Corvus* is Latin for "crow" and *brachyrhynchos* means "short beak." Crows belong to the Corvids, a Latin name for the family that also includes ravens, magpies, and jays, all of which are known for their intelligence. As a group, they are "the top of the line in avian evolution, among the most recent and successful of modern birds," writes Candace Savage in *Bird Brains*. "Their brain-to-body ratio equals that of dolphins and nearly matches our own."

Monogamous creatures that live in extended and cooperative family groups, crows might remind us of ourselves, or of the actions we would have taken had we the chutzpah of crows. Consider, for example, Edgar Allen Crow who, with his family, was out flying along a road one day when he collided with a fast-moving truck. Unbeknownst to Edgar, who was not Edgar at the time, but just crow, there was a witness to the accident, a naturalist named Melanie Marshall who worked at a nearby nature center, and who ran immediately to help the crow. Unbeknownst to Melanie was Edgar's family, who literally were waiting in the wings, or on the wings, their black-caped "Supercrow" wings. For when Melanie attempted to lift Edgar from the hot, dark tar of the street, his family—in their Superman mode of search and rescue—set out to reclaim Edgar from Melanie. They sped from the trees to bomb her with their bodies, all the while cursing, crow-style, at her. What chutzpah was this!? But Melanie pressed on, noticing during the chaos that some of the birds battling her had spots of white on their feathers.

Before too long, Melanie had secured Edgar in her arms and carried him off. As it turned out, he was left flightless and unable to fend for himself after the accident. This made him eligible to become a crow ambassador in Melanie's nature center, to where, she reports, "His family has moved with him. It's clearly his family. Some of them have the same white-spotted feathers. When there are no humans around, they land by him. They visit him. They sit on his outdoor cage. He throws the food we give *him* to *them!*"

In relocating to the grounds of the nature center, Edgar's family understood the crow mantra, which is similar to that of, say, the Mafia's: Family first. This fidelity of one crow to another is common in crow life. Young birds are welcome to stay with their parents and siblings until they decide to move off and establish their own home area. The territory of the parent birds, along with those grown children still living at home, is occupied year-round and for life. In spring and summer, the crow family spends its days and nights near this home, tending to family life, with the young from one or more previous years helping their parents feed and guard the newest brood. In fall and winter, the home area is used during the day, but by late afternoon the family and the larger community of crows migrates to the communal roost.

Before I began my drive along Rockville Pike searching for the crows' most current roosting site, I asked an Audubon Society official if any environmental impact statements were conducted before construction destroyed the Montrose roost I'd seen in 1995. "People knew it was there," the official said, "but crows aren't an endangered species, you know." She snickered.

Why is it we take for granted all but what we are about to lose?

There had been complaints about the Montrose roost, complaints about the noise and that such a large roost—nearly five hundred thousand birds, maybe more—could present health hazards. By 1997, the birds had moved their roost to trees accessorizing the parking lot of White Flint Mall, a large, upscale shopping paradise less than two miles south of Montrose Road. "But," said the Audubon official, "I don't know where they are now."

I remembered the crows at White Flint, perched in feeble trees shoppers had to pass by to enter or leave Lord & Taylor and Bloomingdale's. The problem was that these were not window display birds but real birds. After a movie at the mall during my Christmas visit in 1997, I walked to my car, around 9:30 P.M. A couple hurried by arm in arm, faces down, as though walking by birds was akin to hurrying down a dangerous street. Next to my car, in a truly fragile and skinny parking lot sort of tree, were at least two dozen crows, weighing down the weak branches. Crows are diurnal birds, meaning they are awake during the day and sleep during the night. But these parking lot crows were crows with insomnia, crows attempting to sleep under the bright lights of a mall, and not succeeding. Many were dipping through the night sky, startled by, and perhaps startling, shoppers who, after a day of gathering goods for their own nest of a home, were now migrating out of the mall to go and roost in their own human way. Because folks felt a frightening Hitchcockian flavor to the parking lot at night, the mall began a "roost harassment" program, hoping this would motivate the birds to seek refuge somewhere else. When the harassment calls failed, the mall began "bombing" the roost with firecracker-like sounds. This land, too, was to be exclusive.

Would there have been more tolerance for suburban birds like the beautiful cardinal or robin? Must beauty be a requirement?

With a little empathy, a little anthropomorphism, you could imagine a bomb waking you, shattering the night, imagine the great growing of fear twisting through your muscles. Imagine the dread of fleeing into the peril of the great horned owl at your wingtip. "Anthropomorphism," writes the Jungian psychologist James Hillman, "recognizes that humans and animals participate in a common world of significations. We can and do understand each other despite the arrogant philosophies that would preserve consciousness as an exclusively human property."

In the scientific world anthropomorphism is a crime. Condemned. Laughed at. If I commit any crimes during my life, let them be crimes of passion on behalf of the nonhuman world. My life is in need of such sin.

a   b a n i s h m e n t   o f   c r o w s

. . .

I am no longer a visitor to Maryland. Great blue herons fly over my little stone cottage in a small, old community just outside the northwest border of Washington, D.C. They hunt in the shallows of the Potomac River that rushes furiously along the bottom of the ridge of land to which my husband and I have moved with Madeleine, who is now nearly three years old. Beaver, deer, opossum, and raccoon trek through the Potomac's wooded shoreline; and five-lined skinks scurry along our street and up the stone steps of my front porch.

In New York, the streets were fat with the future—the next great play or dance or idea or job or assignment for me to discover. But Maryland represents to me what the Celts called a "thin place": a geographical location where a person experiences only a very thin divide between past, present, and future. I grew up in and around Rockville; and I will probably die here.

Outside in the mornings, Madeleine and I hear the cawing of crows, at first far away, echoing through the woods along the river. Slowly they close in, spot us throwing corn, bread, and sunflower seeds into the grass, and land in the tall trees around our cottage. Once, a high mound of upturned earth two houses away drew hundreds of crows searching for garbage. The birds covered the roofs of several homes and lined the tree branches. Squinting at the crows through sunlight transformed them into blowsy black scarves of silk, a fabric of crow society Madeleine and I wished to enter. We walked toward them along our stone path; and suddenly they fell silent as we moved below what now felt like a mountain of scrupulous black eyes. It was one of those moments when suddenly you feel you've crossed over the edge of your civilized world and into quite another. The tables turn, then, and you are not doing the turning. If you surrender to it—to the moment when perhaps the wild and tame are one—there's a light in all that black, an openness there at the edge of the question, as you wait to see what answer the world will serve you. Clutched by crows, we were granted the tiniest bit of time before a neighbor passed by walking a noisy dog. The birds swept down, hooked our thoughts, and flew off with them.

"You will find yourself again only in the simple and forgotten things," wrote Jung. I have a clear picture in my mind of when I was twelve. I wore a yellow rain coat, held a pad of paper and a pencil, stood by a wood fence, and watched crows just ten feet away nibbling in my yard. Day after day the crows came to search the grass for food; and I imagined I could tame them if I stayed near long enough, not knowing that perhaps the only reason they stayed at all was because I had yet to be tamed myself.

In returning to Maryland, I have returned to a landscape that sustained not only a roost of hundreds of thousands of crows, but a girl who long ago fell captive to them.

When I think about it, my past consists of hundreds of trips up and down Rockville Pike. In a way, the road maps my childhood and adolescence; the details are delineated along the side streets, in the parking lots, shops, and restaurants. For instance, the one and only McDonald's in the area was, years ago, on the Pike. My parents used to take the family there for dinner and then to the now defunct Rockville Drive-In. My brother, sister, and I watched the children's show before sleeping through the main adult feature in the back of our white station wagon. The Pike is the road on which, in a grocery store, my brother gave me, a two-year-old, an oversized gumball on which I nearly choked to death. It is the same store where, in the parking lot, just before I left for college, I denied my mother's entire existence by arrogantly announcing that I couldn't imagine anyone actually wanting to be a wife and spend her entire life in Rockville. I am now a mother and wife. This is a thin place.

My drive along the Pike to search for the crows begins at 4:45 P.M. at Congressional Plaza, just a stone's throw from the Montrose roost site of 1995. A main attraction at Congressional is Starbucks Coffee. But I remember summers there filled with ice-cream sundaes and surreptitious glances with the first boy who ever unsettled

a   b a n i s h m e n t   o f   c r o w s

me by inadvertently touching my leg with his under a coffee table. We were fifteen. He was the same boy with whom I played basketball and football. In winter he taught me about ice-skating on the ponds and lakes along Rock Creek; and he told me I would be safe as long as I listened to the ice. The cracking of it, he said, sounded different depending on its thickness, its location, the time of day. I believed him and learned to think of ice in terms of its voice—thunderous, brittle, deep, feathery, squeaky.

Before Congressional Plaza was a shopping center it was a local airport. Near the airport, in the 1930s, worked a man who is now eighty-one years old, Mr. Porter Welsh, a southern gentleman who now lives in Florida and is considered by Rockville historians to be part of Rockville's living history. "Of course in the ol' days we didn't think of crows as a problem, just put up with 'em more than you younga' folks," said Porter when I called to ask him, since he is living history, about crows, birds that have a history as well. "When I was a small child," Porter continued, "I knew the sounds of the crows comin' and goin'. Would imagine they've been there for eons. I saw them, dense numbers of 'em behind the old airport. I watched them go out in the mornin' and come back in evenin'. At night, the woods back there were thick with 'em. Land along what is now Montrose and Congressional Plaza, jus' off the Pike, was forest and farmland way back. That's where I saw 'em, in the thirties and forties. They utilized all that area. I would know. I lived there for some years."

I want to know: Are there crows out there with a secret allegiance to the woods their ancestors have flown in and out of for sixty years, as Porter says? Then why not a hundred years, a thousand, or more? Could there be crows with a homeland? I search for the birds believing they have a sense of place and, by consequence of roost harassment and unceasing suburban sprawl, a deep sense of impending placelessness as well.

By 5:00, as I walk out of Starbucks with my favorite coffee, it is nearly time for the train of crows to cross the sky. At first I see a few small groups of crows flying with purpose through the wind and rain, but no black line that I can easily follow to their destination. I get in my car and head south along the Pike, passing by strip mall, strip mall, strip mall. Each stoplight is a chance to look up for a minute or so and think about the birds. Has the weather caused them to disperse? Is a count of twenty or so crows a sure bet to the roost? They fly over the traffic in groups of six, ten, eight. I set off after a group of twelve, which of course I lose after another stoplight. In the traffic it will be impossible to follow a particular group. I park by Toys "R" Us to watch for any pattern to their flying. If more than one group appears to fly in the same general direction, I'll drive in that direction too, without the birds as guides.

I end up on a less-traveled road that intersects the Pike across from White Flint Mall. It feels wrong, but I go anyway. Zipping over the top of a small hill I think I see crows in trees, but I'm driving too fast to be sure and so pull a quick, illegal, U-turn in the middle of the road and head back. Near the trees is a parking lot with a chain slightly raised over the entrance. To get closer to the trees I need to cross over the chain and enter this parking lot, which, after a small debate with myself, I do, figuring that, like the illegal U-turn, this is just another small sin. Nearly immediately, a white van with flashing yellow lights pulls up next to my car. *One of the wonders of security patrols, their appearing out of nowhere,* I think as my stomach feels suddenly in my throat. As the darkened window of the van rolls down, a tiny criminal feeling that is weirdly exciting crawls over me. The patrol behind the window is a bone thin young man, a boy, of maybe seventeen; and he says, rather flimsily, that he is with the White Flint Security Patrol. What am I doing here, he wants to know? Am I an employee for White Flint? This is, after all, he says, the special employee parking lot during the Christmas season.

I lie. Another sin. I tell him I'm a biologist studying bird flight patterns, especially those of crows, which is partially true.

"Oh crows!"

I am in luck—a boy who knows the crows. "Do you know where they are?" I ask.

a b a n i s h m e n t   o f   c r o w s

"Hear those firecrackers? They come from a gun on the roof of the mall," he proudly educates me. "It's to scare the crows. That's why they're flying in all these crazy directions."

This is good. My illegal U-turn and my lies have brought me to this toddler of a security guard, and he has been helpful. I now know why I can't find a black line of crows in the sky that would lead to the roost. I listen to the firecrackers and say, "I didn't think the mall was still bombing the crows."

"People don't like the bird droppings on their cars," he answers. "We start bombing at 5:00 P.M. But I'm usually on the early morning shift. That's when I see the crows flying out. They come," he pauses, "from down there," as he points south.

He accompanies me to the proper exit, at which I thank him before proceeding "down there," a quiet street that parallels the Pike and which is lined on one side with a thin and decorative line of deciduous trees, and on the other side with office buildings that, so close to Christmas, are fairly deserted. Everyone is shopping. The blazing red-scripted sign of Lord & Taylor, at White Flint Mall, is visible from the corner where I park. Rolling down my window to listen for bombs, I quickly notice the heavy sound of scraping feathers; I hear guttural *gwal*s and *op*s; scattered screeches and woodpecker-like rattles. Where are the crows? Next to my car are four tall white pine trees I am ignoring, thinking the birds prefer deciduous trees. But then crows appear. Some wing their way into the pines, while others shoot out, performing aerial gymnastics. The *gwal*s, *op*s, and *caw*s intensify. Inside the pines the birds are identifying themselves and greeting one another, seniors are overthrowing juniors for the interior branch spots, they may even be, some ornithologists believe, exchanging information about area food supplies. All those years ago I had learned to think of ice in terms of its voice. Something similar could now be said of trees.

From that point on, I drive with the window down, listening for what I cannot see. There are maybe only several hundred birds in the trees around the office buildings; this must not be the crows' final roosting site. The bombs stab the air on no apparent schedule;

crows are smart enough to recognize a pattern, which might lessen their fear, which might lead them to return to the mall to roost. I decide to leave this little warzone in search of the bigger roost. It is 5:23.

By 5:30 I am back in the Toys "R" Us parking lot. Scanning the sky, I see nothing and so decide to give up and take the Pike to go grocery shopping. This turns out to be a good idea. Stuck in traffic at one of the busiest intersections in Rockville, that of Montrose and the Pike, I hear a raucous crow symphony playing in a struggling band of trees. I peer into the dark trees and see, somehow, thousands of crows silhouetted against the sky. I decide to call this spot roost #1, for lack of something more creative, and turn with the green light at the corner to find a parking lot from which to watch the birds. It is 5:43.

I pull into a smear of asphalt surrounding a historic Rockville site, the little schoolhouse called Montrose School, built in 1909. It is no longer a school and is, in fact, vacant—a meaningless structure lost in the thousands of more modern structures around it. It is a relic, something that would have been significant in Porter's life. Though this leads me to think the building may have meaning to the crows, in a collective avian unconscious way, a vestigial image from old crow culture—when the building was a white dot on the then primarily forested land, a building to fly toward, a landmark on the way to the roost. There are crows in the thin trees around the school. In fact, there are birds flying from roost #1 to these trees by the school, what I will call roost #2. It is strangely quiet here. Just a few rattles and caws from the birds. Even the traffic seems far off, which it is not. The springlike smell of the December rain washes over me, and I am stained with a sadness for these birds, for their losses.

By 6:00 P.M. it is dark. I look behind me toward the harshly lit parking lot—a parking lot with lights so extremely bright they approximate daylight in the night—and I realize I am near the store wherein I choked on the gumball. I look up to the sky and am startled to see seagulls flocking. When I was a kid, seagulls lived only at the shore; they were a highlight of summer vacations at the beach, three hours away from here. As I put the car into gear, I see crows leaving roost #1 for roost #2. When they fly into the bright beams of the parking lot lights, their undersides radiate white, which is when I understand it was not seagulls I had seen just a few minutes before, but crows, crows sparkling. White crows in a black sky. Once again the tables have turned; for a few seconds crows are angels; the world is inside out.

I am back at the intersection by 6:04. Above the red, yellow, and green lights fly more crows. They do not scatter but move together, across the Pike, and I follow them to another parking lot, where they drop quietly into the few surviving trees of the Montrose roost. The easternmost corner, where traffic drones on around them. Construction trailers, temporary fencing, a sign for ADC Builders and PBM Mechanical—these things litter the street alongside the roost. Will the next few months be the last months of this landscape? It is only a fragment of what it was once; but nevertheless it is the crows' landscape, their historic roosting site, their place.

Suddenly, with the wind, the smell of butter and fresh-baked bread wafts over from a nearby strip mall where there is a bakery called La Madeleine.

The crows, my daughter. My daughter, the crows. I get out of my car to walk through the twisting rain and dark, empty parking lot alongside the madness of the crows' lives. With their final banishment from this spot so also will disappear any secret allegiance they have had, for hundreds, maybe thousands, of years to this land. Of course the crows will find a new roost, but they will not land here when Madeleine is old enough to understand the significance of their soaring to and from their sacred homeland.

Meanwhile, Madeleine will grow up and learn to count, *One for sorrow, two for joy . . . seven for the secret of the crows never to be told.*

The Hopes of Snakes

Jesus saith, Ye ask who are those that draw us to the
kingdom... ? The fowls of the air, and all beasts that
are under the earth or upon the earth, and the fishes
of the sea, these are they which draw you....
The Sayings of Jesus, second saying

It was the season of wind, wind undressing the trees, trees dropping
their gold, lime and ruby red lingerie of leaves to the gasping fields
of an old farm where, on this particular day, an Oktoberfest celebration was underway. Chimney smoke and the scent of roasting
chestnuts swept through the people strolling along in the seductive
arms of the cool, smooth air. Wagons of pumpkins and gourds,
hawks, the fattening hedgehogs eating farther out in the fields—
these were welcome accessories to the day, signs of autumn people
pointed out and stood still to see. Things embraced. But a snake—
a snake migrating toward the darker doors of the earth, down to the
hotter core of things to wrap itself like a winter scarf around the
cold, dry bodies of other snakes—would be unwelcome. On this
afternoon, though, a snake did slide out of the woods and with it
came the biggest question of the day: Who would kill the snake?

Who would wrestle with the six feet of muscle that slithered
neatly under the people and around the legs of tables set up to sell
crafts and food on this festive occasion? That the unease over the
snake was disproportionate to the actual danger of the creature was
not relevant. The concern seemed to be: Who does this snake think
it is, venturing out of the trees to travel into the open grasses where

stood people just now realizing the snake by their feet was not a child's toy but an actual live serpent? People perhaps seeing a snake of such size for the first time in their lives.

Of course there are those who would argue that the snake did not, could not, in any way decide anything at all. Those who would contend that although a snake can see quite well—not just lightness and darkness but actual images—it could not have considered what was before it: weekend visitors who just hours ago this very happy afternoon had fled the confines of their suburban homes to arrive at this island of farmland. Certainly, people had come to the park with thoughts of apple fritters and cider on their minds. They did not have as part of their plan for the day a meeting with what, I believed, as I watched the chaos mount, to be a black rat snake— a nonvenomous, daytime prowler that can grow longer than six feet and, in comparison with other North American snakes, meets the criteria for being a near giant in the United States.

Someone ran for a park naturalist who was last seen moseying around the candle-maker's table. The naturalist arrived with an apparent lack of conviction over what was to be done to this obviously magnanimous snake sunning and resting itself along its itinerary. By the time the snake continued moving, seemingly determined to get somewhere but confused—*what is all this in my way?*—there had been time to see that, yes, it was a horse of a snake in the grass; a black beauty of a rat snake.

Soon enough the naturalist poked her walking stick in front of the snake, assuming that such action would turn the snake back to its dark and leafy woodland. But the snake was persistent in its plans and the naturalist's annoying stick that blocked the snake over and over again caused the animal to rear up in an effort to find a way around the obstacle. This rearing up, this show of its intent —or, as the crowd understood it, this show of the snake's absolute anger—heightened the anxiety of the crowd and a certain controlled panic set in. It wasn't that people were possessed with erratic yelling and jumping; rather it was an unease displayed with various body languages. Some people stomped and then rubbed their feet into the ground in a circular motion (as though perhaps the snake could be squished); others began gathering sticks and large rocks (as apparently the snake could be "sticked and stoned" to death); children—boys, especially—fashioned their hands into guns and fired off a few rounds. The whole scene conjured up images of what I imagined as prehistoric humans preparing for the sacrifice. It was as though the autumn winds had summoned all the rage against and fear of snakes throughout the ages and imparted it to these otherwise innocent and festive-seeking citizens, of which one, or a few, would be chosen to kill the serpent at their feet.

In what seems now like another life, since it was so long ago, when I was eight, my alcoholic aunt Sissy used to say that I was "patient as a snake." Though I think she said this more with the intention of exposing me as a sneaky little kid, since I enjoyed surreptitiously watching her from the overstuffed, rose-patterned wingback chair as she flitted about my great grandmother's apartment singing and dancing—unlike my other more composed Irish-Catholic relatives—I rather liked being compared to a snake. Back then, as a newly minted Catholic having recently made my first confession and communion, I was aware of patience. "Patience of spirit is better than haughtiness of spirit. . . . Ecclesiastes 7:8–9," my Sunday school teacher often quoted to us, her students. Or, "Wait for the LORD; be strong and let your heart take courage; yes, wait for the LORD," the teacher would sometimes yell out as we fought over who got what few colors of crayons there were, leaving us to guess that her directive perhaps meant the Lord was making more crayons for us. In the end, as much as I was educated on the virtues of patience, I knew more about it not from confession, communion, Sunday school, or church, but from an actual snake.

Not long before I'd had the privilege of watching my aunt in her "Irish revelry," as my great-grandmother used to call it, I had come upon a large, thick-bodied, and coiled snake on a rocky, wooded hillside near my home in what was then a somewhat remote area of Massachusetts. A friend and my younger sister were

the hopes of snakes

with me. In those days, children were set loose. My mother—in the ways of her mother and, I would guess, all my foremothers—pitched us out of the house when it was sunny and she had things to do. On the weekends, if there was no visit scheduled to the homes of the happy Irish relatives, or if church slipped by, I spent the morning exploring the landscape of wherever we happened to be living. After lunch and until dinner I busied myself with the slow movements of land snails under the bushes, with the way wild grass grew so long that it fell over into soft cushions, unlike the manicured straight grass of the yard. Sometimes I sat on the porch staring at nothing, which, I can say in retrospect, was everything. Years passed and eventually my curfew meant coming in shortly after the streetlamps came on. If it was summer I was home by nine.

Countless times I've thought about the snake on the hill in Massachusetts. I can remember it so clearly that it could've been yesterday...and I am running with my sister and friend along a path through the forest where ahead of us a thick snake is coiled in a patch of sunlight. I am sticky with the forest, though I cannot say now if the trees are budding and growing or browning and dying. We stop because this is the first wild snake we've seen, ever. I am aware that snakes, like all wild animals, bite when threatened. But the light pouring through the trees and onto the snake is inviting, as though one sunray has been made for this one snake. The animal's long body of brown and gray and beige is drenched in yellow air. We are curious.

At the time, snakes were, simply, snakes, as our cat was our cat. That this snake did not hear well but instead picked up vibrations (such as our running) from the ground, that it had a highly developed sense of smell and through its forked tongue could taste the odors of our young sweating bodies—all of this I never conceived of. We circled the coiled snake, believing that when it lifted its head from the pillows of its body and then fell back into itself, it saw us and was not bothered.

Much later in my life I learned that the way snakes and other animals, including humans, see or perceive their environment

the hopes of snakes

depends on each animal's sensory capabilities. This is known as *"umwelt,"* a German expression that, loosely translated, means "the world around me." Essentially, the reality of one's world is determined differently for different species.

Freud once said something similar: "No one lives in the real world," he announced. Another writer, Willard Gaylin, says "We occupy a space of our own creation—a collage compounded by bits and pieces of actuality arranged into a design determined by our internal perceptions, our hopes, our fears, our memories, and our anticipations."

My perception of the snake on the hill is that it was, if not friendly, then, tolerant, permissive. It appeared patient; and so we decided to double back up the path to get a running start on leaping into the yellow light, over the snake. We jumped. And jumped again. Eventually, we left.

Some evenings now I am convinced that I've identified this old snake—that it was an Eastern hognose snake, or a milk snake, or a timber rattlesnake. All three species could have lived on that hill. Though from my memory the milk snake seems a bit too slender and silvery, and though the hognose snake really should have played dead (as hognose snakes are known to do when approached), logic is in their favor because we were not bitten, as is the assumed rattlesnake response.

The truth is that any of the three species could have struck us. The truth, I know now, is that snakes often are sleepy and dismissive soon after they emerge from hibernation and set out to warm themselves in the spring sunshine. Even the timber rattlesnake is known to be mild-mannered and to remain quietly coiled when approached.

I roll these truths over my tongue, but the knowledge has taken me only so far. Attempting to determine the species of this snake has, it seems, been the wrong question all these years. If there is truth to what the Hopi Indians believe—that snakes bring to humans the message of the hills—then the appropriate question is: what is the message?

the hopes of snakes

. . .

It is said that only those who forget why they came to this world will lose their way. I thought of this as I headed out of Manhattan during one of my last autumns in the city to meet a man who was reintroducing reptiles and amphibians to an abandoned airfield on the outskirts of Brooklyn.

When I had first called Bob Cook to offer my assistance with his project, he asked, "Why the hell does a girl from Manhattan want to muck around finding snakes with a scientist in Brooklyn?" Too embarrassed to say that I was looking for a mentor of sorts, someone to teach me how to hold snakes—and figuring I already should have this one skill for this specific job—I avoided the question by babbling on about the fact that he and I had had the same herpetology professor in graduate school at New York University, and that indeed it was this professor who had referred me to him.

I neglected to tell him that my experience with wild snakes was limited to the one I'd seen in Massachusetts some twenty-five years before. Explaining to him—a man of science and reason—that, increasingly, over the last ten years of living in New York, my old snake from Massachusetts kept prowling through my memory. Explaining to him that as many times as I had tried to disregard the event as a silly childhood memory, or invention even, since it seemed, as I'd grown up, to have been quite an improbable occurrence, that the snake nevertheless lurked in the backcountry of my mind. I left all this out, guessing such details would work against his hiring me, which he did by hanging up with, "Yeah, see you."

It was now October, and since late September I had been helping Bob locate turtles with radio-telemetry. The time had come, though, to find the snakes, black racers, which were not outfitted with any radio-tracking devices. They were migrating toward their hibernaculum for the winter. Locating the snakes, Bob said, would be more difficult than finding the turtles, and more dangerous. "I hope you'll be at least as much help to me as my dog," he joked with me, "which isn't that much." Bob's dog, Gus, was a black lab that failed out of an ivy-league pheasant-hunting school for dogs in

Maine and so was recruited and trained by Bob in the alternate activity of locating reptiles, turtles mostly, though Gus explored the snake-lands with us.

Five years before Bob had released the black racers, garter snakes, painted turtles, box turtles, and an assortment of other amphibians onto this old airfield in Brooklyn with the goal of creating a permanent home for them on what is their ancestral homeland, which happens also to be one of the last tracts of coastal estuarine environments in New York City. For each of the past four years he has had the difficult job of relocating and catching the animals he freed in order to see which have lived, which have been wounded, and which have died.

The landscape we searched is a place defined mostly by what one does not think of as New York City. The skyscrapers of Manhattan dissolve in the sky between there and here; the wind is salty and scented of marsh and mud; the calls of sparrows, gulls, cardinals, and finches drizzle down to us in those moments between the take-offs and landings of planes from JFK Airport; marsh grasses chafe against one another in such masses that they appear to be dancing and humming at once. There is color here—sharp blues of an open, autumn sky; tawny browns and beiges of cattails and phragmites; simmering oranges, reds, and yellows of leaves and cherry and bayberry bush thickets, as though this landscape is a stew of what the earth has been hungering for since Brooklyn became Brooklyn.

New York—this is no city for snake-lovers. "In thickly populated areas such as our city, the worst enemies of the resident snakes are the human inhabitants," writes John Kiernan in *A Natural History of New York City*. "Why almost everyone's hand is against them is an age-old question to which I never have heard a good and sufficient answer." I think of New Yorkers and snakes, of how our awareness and direct experience of serpents is so limited that what we believe about them functions as a sort of anti-knowledge. In the absence of contact, the snake's life forms in the human mind as a nightmare of slithering, of fangs, of constriction, of venom, of being swallowed slowly, and in full.

It is said that people fear snakes because we fear the primitive brain activity associated with our own reptile brain—that part of our brain that we have in common with the brains of reptiles and which is known as the limbic system. This system sets in motion our defense mechanisms and triggers our instincts to flee or fight, to save ourselves from any perceived dangers or threats. If humans do indeed fear this part of themselves, then our fear of snakes is based on the fear of the snake within, rather than on any direct experience of snakes. All of that seems a bit murky and entirely unconscious. Another theory, according to Gordon M. Burghardt and Harold A. Herzog in their article "Animals, Evolution, and Ethics," is that "snakes readily access trees—man's old habitat—and certain species are poisonous and deadly. . . . Thus we see no problem in ascribing the fear of snakes . . . to genetic factors." This seems more plausible. Though as I search for the black racers, I wonder, too, if the fear of snakes is associated with the definition of the word "cold-blooded." The fact that a snake's body is "cold-blooded" seems largely ignored when compared to the common understanding of the word as a behavior or an action taken without consideration, compunction, or clemency. Essentially, the state of being cold-blooded is equated with being emotionless. The idea is that not only do snakes kill, but that they do it cold-bloodedly.

Bob whistles for me to follow him in the same way he whistles for his dog and, like Gus, I move quickly and with my tail between my legs. Black racers, Bob has told me, are in a league of their own in terms of the ferocity with which people view them. A racer is a snake with an attitude. Irate. Irascible. Quick-tempered. Vicious.

The shape and size of a snake's teeth vary among species, but typically the teeth are elongated, curve backward, and are tipped with sharp points. A victim's struggle to release itself from a snake's bite causes the snake to deepen the penetration of its teeth, which essentially are grasping tools. The rearward curve of the teeth ensures that the snake disengages the prey only as the victim is shuttled toward the rear of the snake's mouth.

Contrary to popular belief, the black racer does not chase humans. Instead, humans—at least those who are interested in catching a racer—do the chasing. Racers, with their large eyes and good eyesight, glide quickly, with their head raised off the ground, and they often vanish just as they are noticed. The herpetologist C. H. Pope once said that "snakes are first cowards, next bluffers, and last of all warriors." If a racer is approached suddenly and its route of escape—escape being what it prefers to do—is cut off, the racer will defend itself. Bob tells me that if I hesitate at all to catch the racer when I find it that the snake will raise up and strike me repeatedly with its open and endless mouth.

Bob finds a certain enjoyment in frightening me, I think as I walk through the fields remembering the first day I met him, when his words to me were little more than "hello" and "here, put on these chest-waders." He then drove me to a man-made pond that previously had functioned as a trash dump. I stepped out of the truck. He handed me a six-foot-long stick and told me to wave it through the pond to hit on the wire cage traps he'd left partially submerged in the water for the painted turtles he'd released and was attempting to recapture. If I found a trap, I was to bring it up and haul it out. The job sounded easy enough, until, as I was on my way into the pond, Bob warned me of four things. One, the pond once was a dump; watch out for the broken glass. Two, don't slam the snapping turtles that may reside in the pond; they have a vicious and powerful bite. Three, the water would be over my head in places, though, where, exactly, he did not know. Finally, the mud worked much like quicksand; should I start to sink, raise the stick over my head. He would find me when he returned. All of this as he breezed away over a hill to another pond.

While I thought about retreating, I walked into the pond, remembering what Carl Jung once said: "The irrational fullness of life has taught me never to discard anything, even when it . . . admits of no immediate explanation. It is of course disquieting, . . . but security, certitude, and peace do not lead to discoveries."

There are times when, somehow, you know to trust because you sense what could be: your own revealing, your own unerring move-ment toward intention and awareness.

Bob inspired such trust. It wasn't that he talked or smiled much or was even that companionable. He consistently left me trailing behind him; and when I caught up he was already talking to a tur-tle, swallowing in the late-day sun, or sniffing a handful of soil near the fragrant bayberry bushes. Bob was like several people from my past, people who knew that we begin dying as soon as we are born, and so believed in living with impulse and sincerity; but damn the courtesies. For them, life was a series of doors: doors of opportunity, of doubt, even doors of fear. Imagine these doors scattered in the forests, in the seas, in the air. Sailing through a hail storm, the is-land of St. John disappearing, could be a door, depending on how you look at it. Tip-toeing through a secretive, dark, and wet pan-ther cave in Guatemala?—a door. There may be an open door in the thousand turbulent waters of mating South American fur seals, as well as one in a shark-infested cove in the Galápagos, in the endless turquoise clouds over Borneo. Enter a door and you enter the mys-terious and the unpredictable; you unfold; your body unites with the world; and your pounding heart can be nothing other than your faith.

Bob's door was this land laced with snakes and snapping turtles, this seeming wasteland of New York City. He'd brought life back to the old airfield. Here in Brooklyn he'd grown his own Garden of Eden, to which I'd come knocking, and he had let me in.

I catch up with Bob in a field where he previously has left large boards, pieces of metal, and old blankets, under which he believes the snakes will be hiding. "Find a snake, catch it," he reminds me. My *umwelt,* my world at this moment, is not Bob's *umwelt.* We are walking through the same field, but while he's handled dozens of snakes, I am hesitant and fearful. I've still to feel the skin of even one snake against my own. The wild snake from Massachusetts hangs in the branches of my mind, as though, like Eve, I am being drawn toward something.

the hopes of snakes

After twenty minutes Bob yells across the field that he's found a snake. I stop to watch as he gently guides the snake into a pillowcase to examine it later. Maybe this will be easy, as soft and welcoming as a pillowcase.

We separate and twenty minutes more pass. "Anything?" he yells out as he walks toward me.

"No."

"Women," he says, exasperated.

"Lift this metal board here. There'll be some."

I've been avoiding this metal board. I know that as soon as the board is lifted I will have only seconds before the snakes either race away or fight. I don't want to hesitate and lose them. Nonetheless, I grab the corner of the board and toss it back to find three coiled black racers. Because I fail to move quickly, they see us, lift up out of their coils, strike out, and slap their tails in a defensive maneuver intended to sound like a rattlesnake.

"Grab one! Behind the head!" Bob yells.

I lunge down closer to the earth, squint my eyes, and throw my hand into the rattling racers to catch one. Bob grabs the other two and quickly yet gently begins to examine them. Awkward and afraid, I impatiently dangle my three-foot-long racer in the air at an arm's length from my body. Sharp pricks of the snake's teeth clamp first into my hand near my thumb and then into the fleshy outer edge. I hold on, expecting more bites as the snake thrashes its body erratically, hysterically, slapping against my arm and discharging a thick, white, foul-smelling, cream-like substance that smudges down the long sleeve of my tee shirt.

Bob releases his racers and takes mine to soothe it. I was holding it wrong, he snarls at me: "You suspend a snake in the air and it will bite you. Snakes don't like to fly. They relate to the world by being in contact with it. People fear the snake is going to strangle them, but it's just trying to get close—they're very tactile creatures."

The racer settles on Bob's bare white arm for a few minutes. He motions to me to roll up my sleeve as he lifts my arm next to his. The snake gently slithers from Bob's body to mine. It is calm now and its skin is soft like fine leather. The snake wraps its body around my arm from my elbow to my hand, as intimate as a lover. It rests its strong, black face on my fingers and with the flaring forth of its tongue begins to know me.

Goethe said: "Every object well-contemplated creates an organ for its perception." Since moving from New York to Maryland, snakes, mostly injured or dead, pour into my life. Notes from my journals:

> • A park naturalist at Black Hills found a black rat snake on a rock. The snake had been poked with dozens of pins, including one in the snake's eye, which over the past few days had shriveled away. The naturalist told me of his plans to rehabilitate the snake, though he was worried. If he released a one-eyed snake it would be an easier target for more abuse. Although he seemed resigned to this fact, I could tell it made him sad. Before he walked away he said, "Did you know snakes don't cry?"
>
> • A friend of my sister's told me he shot two big snakes (doesn't know what kind) on his property on the eastern shore of Maryland. He was waiting to ambush them. When they emerged into the sun from a hole in the ground, he put a rifle to their heads. "Ain't good for nothin'" is how he described the snakes; and I countered that they were good for eating rodents. "Ain't no rodents on my property," he shrugged. There was nothing more I could say to him. I left feeling as Wittgenstein must have when he said: "What we cannot speak about we must pass over in silence."
>
> • Neighbor down the street has snakes in the basement. Not sure what species. The housekeeper found the snakes and sprayed them with chemicals from her cleaning bottles. When the snakes stopped moving, housekeeper bashed them with the broomstick and put them in a plastic grocery bag. I asked the housekeeper to call me if there are any more snakes, though I'm not sure what I would do.

- Again, neighbor's housekeeper kills snakes. She didn't believe I really would come to see the snakes. I came. She opened the grocery bag. Two harmless little brown—and now headless— snakes. Their cold blood was as red as my warm blood.

- A mighty black rat snake was sunning itself on the stone wall of the house today. At first, as I walked up the path toward the front door, I thought somehow the stone had cracked above the water spigot. But as I came closer, the crack was shiny, and it moved! A snake—a snake of some nobility, it seemed, being so big. It dropped down to the garden and hugged the stone, retreating quickly toward the north side of the house. It moved so confidently along the contours of the wall that I could see it has loved this house for a long time. In the backyard, the snake headed straight under the wood deck. Though it was difficult to see by then, I caught glimpses of its body swimming along the top of the soil as it headed for the slit in the old brick porch that, because it never was demolished, is still beneath the deck. A perfect underworld, that, as far as I can tell, must lead to the king's chambers somewhere between the dining room floor and the basement ceiling.

- Early this morning on my walk the boys waiting for the school bus were laughing. On the road was a near-dead, thin green snake. The center of its satiny body was oozing onto the road. I didn't know how to kill it with dignity, without appearing to be one of the boys. So I stroked its delicate, leaf-green body and thought about the joy of its morning, this morning before this moment, when it rippled through the trees, like green rain.

At the Oktoberfest celebration, people hovered near the black rat snake in the field, as did I, until, inexplicably, and without any mindfulness on my part, my legs began walking toward it. My heart was pounding with uncertainty and fear. Soon enough, I was standing above and somewhat behind the snake. Hands that were my hands—hands that had in the past been bitten vigorously by a snake—were at the same time not my hands, in the sense that I did not think about any precise second when it might be best to pick up the snake, or even how to pick up the snake.

the hopes of snakes

And then, in a moment, as in the way a breeze can stir out of nowhere, my heart went calm when I lifted the snake up close to my chest and guided its long black body around my arm, where the snake rested patiently. He was a giant, and at times heavy and awkward as parts of him occasionally slipped off my arm and I had to nudge him back up with my torso. Through crowds of people and quite a long way across the grass and back to a woodpile by the edge of the autumn forest we went.

Trying to make sense out of it all now, I am reminded of what the poet W. G. Sebald wrote: "Our brains . . . are always at work on some quivers of self-organization, however faint, and it is from this that an order arises, in places beautiful and comforting. . . ."

Perhaps, I think sometimes—and find it comforting to think so —that I don't live in the real world, as Freud had said. Maybe I occupy a world nuanced with the hopes of snakes, as though the message is that any of us, with our pounding hearts of faith, could be the messenger for whatever it is that draws us. Of course I never can say for sure; but there are things that happen, and this is how it was.

Take the Long Way Home

If you love it enough, anything will talk with you.
George Washington Carver

Twenty years ago my family moved to the piedmont region of the Maryland countryside, where my parents built a house in a field of crushed cornstalks. The land we came to live on was part of a 110,000-acre agricultural reserve, some of which borders an isolated mountain called Sugarloaf Mountain. On weekend afternoons in our new country, my younger sister and I headed into the long, gold, and rolling autumn land. It was a place bereft of people our age—fourteen and sixteen—and so we came home earlier than expected, our brown hair smelling of hay and chimney smoke.

My friendship with one person, though, Mr. Boyd, grew with the passing of many mornings. Early mornings, when I drove along the road leading out of our field and toward my high school of privilege in the city, I saw Mr. Boyd lingering in the purple light with jugs of water he'd filled from a stream. We began by waving hello.

One winter afternoon when the corn had died, I walked through the gray, crisp, and low-lying fields to Mr. Boyd's place to bring him Christmas cookies and three pairs of thick white socks (because I never saw him wear socks) for so graciously agreeing to be the subject of my junior-year photo essay. He invited me into the darkness of his one-room white house. It was a house passed on to him from his grandparents, who were born into slavery on the plantation land on which my parents had built our home, and from his mother, who, he tried to remember, gave birth to him sometime in the 1890s. He guessed he was eighty-six.

Inside Mr. Boyd's house, I sat at a messy table wet from the water jugs on it, and near enough to a pail of liquid containing what I could smell was Mr. Boyd's urine. I loaded my film by candle-light. He had no electricity, no running water, no bathroom. He lit a fire in his fireplace and apologized for the stacks of bean cans in the corner, for the piles of newspapers and old books, for the chill of his home. After a time, we took photos and ate cookies. The con-fectioners' sugar smeared on his dark cheeks. We talked of deer in the woods behind his house and of the afternoon sun rolling down the flanks of Sugarloaf Mountain out his window.

Despite our good conversation, I felt misplaced. I was a white girl from the suburbs talking to a slave's descendant living in slave quarters. I had land and money but no rural skills. Mr. Boyd had rural skills but no land or money. Country life, I admitted to him, was not in my family tree. I knew nothing about soil or mountains, about crops, about selling eggs and pork on the roadside, about wild animals or the smell of my skin splashed with field dust and sweat. He listened, sighed, said, "Take the long way home and, sooner or later, it will all echo in your body."

I did not know it on that day, but Mr. Boyd and I would remain friends for two years, until I left for college. He died while I was away. What follows is a good-bye letter to him, written now, eigh-teen years after last I saw him.

Dear Mr. Boyd,

You once insisted that there was no freedom like the freedom Sugar-loaf Mountain offered. I was young then and perhaps because I had not been confined, dominated, impeded, hampered, or restricted, I considered myself ineluctably free already. I would come to know Sugarloaf—its shady trails; its sharp outlines in the green air and its soft body muted in the gray rain; its awkwardness as one lone mountain rising out of farmland, like "the tallest kid in class every-one teases," you used to say. But freedom, to me at least, meant leaving the mountain and its surrounding rural farmland behind. Freedom was walking away, not walking within.

the hopes of snakes

The day we hiked to the rural route, from where there was, and still is, an unobstructed view of the mountain, you spoke of freedom again. You recalled walking, as a young, strong man, the miles to Sugarloaf as a tribute to your grandparents who, tethered to their fields, could only dream of rising into mountain air. Perhaps I responded with comments I thought empathic, something about abolition or the Civil War learned in a high school history course. In any case, you said I was born to have so much, you said I would search for freedom because I was privileged to do so, but that it would elude me unless I made a life on the piedmont by Sugarloaf. What kind of freedom was that, I laughed?

You promised then that we would go to the mountain together, promised to show me the freedom. But the hot mornings passed, the geese, the snows. Until finally it was simply that your legs were best suited to loitering in the flatter lands surrounding Sugarloaf. After you died, I had a dream you were homeless on your mountain, where you wandered like the Chinese mountain hermit and poet Han-shan, who centuries ago wrote, "Already it seems like years and years. / Freely drifting, I prowl the woods and streams / And linger watching things themselves."

My hope was to hike Sugarloaf in a rain of fall's warm colors. But things didn't work out until a following spring when I piled my clan of left-wing friends—idealists interested in things like zoology, art, and journalism—into an old blue Pontiac, turned up the Neil Young tape and headed for the mountain. They envisioned Sugarloaf as a twelve-hundred-foot-high peak surrounded by other mountains, rather than the monadnock it is. As we drove closer and closer to the mountain, it began to disappear into itself, to spread, as though lowering its limbs for our climb. We hiked along the Northern Peaks trail and the Mountain Loop that afternoon, imagining the ghosts of the mountains that once stood alongside Sugarloaf, the former sisters of an ancient higher landscape long since eroded into rolling foothills and farmland. Clinging in every dark or luminous niche along our hike was the mountain's blood—a lifeblood, an alchemical blend of oak and cardinal; acorn, maple, chipmunk, and rainwater; mushroom, moss, raccoon scat, and red ant. Several fast hours later and nearing the top, we surfaced through lightning-stunted oak trees and gray boulders skinned with lichen, into the mountain's breath.

Back then I didn't have the experience to support what I am about to say, Mr. Boyd, and forgive me for what you may consider a certain forthrightness. But I am remembering those evenings we watched the sun set behind the mountain, those evenings when I saw the silhouette of Sugarloaf drape feminine curves across the darkening sky. Later I read that the Chinese associate mountains with men—dry, hard, and bright; and they associate water with women—wet, soft, and dark. But being a woman now, and knowing a woman's body, its glens and rhythms, I must side with my initial image of the mountain as female. And I am tempted to embody it with a woman's ways: the climbing of the mountain's topography like the arduous ascent of giving birth—pain, relief, shock, more and more pain; the mountain's shape as the nursing and ravaged breast.

But this is now, and I speak from a somewhat weathered self, as well as a more molded version of who you knew so long ago. Today, I go to Sugarloaf to inhale the yellowness of wet leaves in the way a mother lives off the sweet smell of her baby's skin. Or I go to the mountain to caress her wrinkled paths. In the days of my leftist friends, though, the purist pleasure was conquering the climb and savoring the aftertaste of stretched muscles and scratched bones. I still can picture my friend Debbie up there, attempting to envision Sugarloaf at the bottom of an ancient inland sea, a tidbit of knowledge passed from you to me to her. Meanwhile, Maureen spent the afternoon searching for any unlikely chestnuts, seedlings of the great trees that in your lifetime died away. Laura leapt between patches of the erosion-resistant white quartzite that caps Sugarloaf, looking like a butterfly flittering between bowls of sugar. Mark played his guitar in the tall breezes. And I looked eastward, toward our road, trying to spot your old house. But I did not feel freedom in the way I think you meant. I was free from school—because I'd

skipped out on my responsibilities for a day. Though I remember
you didn't equate escape with freedom.

Wind? Was your freedom in the wind, in the air, because it is
limitless? Because air rushes into the rivers of our bodies, offering,
miraculously, life? Because it offers, invisibly, the sounds of the
world? Because it offers, seamlessly, a blue fabric stitched with
flying birds? Or did freedom come with standing high above the
valley floor but just beneath your image of God, or Heaven? Was it
in an immeasurable pleasure of being the tiniest bit closer to the
sun? In college, when my biology professor lectured on energy and
said sunlight flows through all living things before dispersing back
into space, never to come our way again, I thought of you, Mr.
Boyd. Was freedom being part of the endless energy of the mountain, of the universe?

You had science books in your house, and poetry and fiction,
some history. But philosophers, you believed, complicated the
world. Most valuable was the book of the land. So we walked
through pages of hills, words of trees. You underscored the smell
of wet hay on rainy mornings and the froggy-wet woods by your
house. When the soft chill of the night wrapped around our bodies
like silk, we listened to the music of spring peepers behind the old
plantation mansion and spied on the great horned owl resting on
a television antenna in the moonlight. How many times did we
search with flashlights down by the stone bridge, Sugarloaf on the
horizon, for the eyes of deer and fox stirring like restless stars in
pastures? Your book taught me to feel my blood rush, to feel my
senses heighten as some nocturnal creature myself. But back then
the agricultural preserve with its strong mountain was more the
setting of some novel or children's story than a place to become a
person of some success. What chance did I stand there?

A philosopher I read in college, Norman O. Brown, had an interpretation of freedom. He described it as "an invitation to the
dance; a temptation, or irritation. No satisfying solutions; nothing
to rest in; nothing to weigh us down." This definition was more
concrete than yours, easier to follow. And so I did.

After college, I moved away to New York City, traveled and met men who declared freedom. Men like Eli, who took me twenty-five miles into the Atlantic on a rickety motorized rowboat to have a picnic on a barrier reef island with a Central American fisherman, a chicken, and a dog named Tondo. Men like Harold, who swam with my hand in his as we snorkeled around coral, searching for moray eels. Like Skye, who insisted we get out of our tent to sit on a log in a violent Vermont storm, while he made dinner and laughed, "Ahhh, rain, don't you love it!?" Like the Antarctic sailor in Patagonia who took me through sixty-mile-an-hour winds and shifting icebergs so we could chip ice off a glacier for our vodka. Cheers. Like Carlos, who led me through a jungle of howler monkeys, convinced me to sit in their spray and wait, because soon, he promised, they would howl for us. These men split me open to the world. You told me to stay home.

Random images from my days on Sugarloaf coursed through me while I was away. Leaves scraping in the winds of an Ecuadorian rain shower announced the familiar roar of Sugarloaf's stormy canopy. And a condor flying the Chilean Andes cut the sky like the turkey vulture whose black shadow slid across my shoulders on top of our mountain. I missed our land then, remembering the astonishment of being momentarily subsumed by the great wings of a bird's solitary flight. Then, on a day on the other side of the world, I saw dwelling in drips of Borneo's rain forest all the sunspots Sugarloaf ever invented. Even a late-night walk home from work along the streets of Manhattan took me back to the mountain. Muffled behind the harsh slaps of my heeled footsteps on city concrete, I heard my hiking boots resonating on Sugarloaf's trails—a gentle pat, a small echo, a tiny absorption of the body into the earth.

But life had been calling since long before my travels. The slick media with its advertising, MTV, and endless cable television stations depicted an increasingly self-interested, self-promoted, self-enriched idea of what it meant to be young and American. News events chronicled a conflicted and disappearing world. My bohemian friends and I would jump into it all. We would be zoologists

the hopes of snakes

saving primates in Indonesia, journalists on the front line of injustice in Central America, photographers snapping images of vanishing wildlife in the Hebrides. We would find honor in rootlessness.

Fed by dreams of rescuing the larger world, I was oblivious to the possibility that Sugarloaf itself needed saving. I guess the land of one's childhood is akin to the room of one's childhood: you assume your treasures will always be there and are surprised to come home to find the room redecorated. Do not be afraid, Mr. Boyd, your mountain still stands. But the designation of the land surrounding the mountain as an agricultural preserve does not leave it invincible. Corn now grows in the air of the coal-burning power plant in Sugarloaf's valley. And it grows among radioactive soil particles that, despite community outrage and complaint, continue to leak from a nuclear production facility near the mountain's base. The most recent threat to Sugarloaf is a proposed highway that would cut through the preserve near the mountain. Meant to ease traffic congestion between northern Virginia and rural Maryland, the road, should it be built, would ravage the preserve with development and yet more traffic. In the effort to ease, we ultimately dis-ease.

Mr. Boyd, you left me in a world drunk with the ideas of success, excess, progress.

Of course, I hopped on for the ride. Consumed with the heady bivouac that feminism provided, I believed the theory that freedom, liberation, and personal success could best be found by foregoing certain things—namely marriage and motherhood, at least for a time. It would be negligent, unfair, and arrogant to say I could've done without the privileges passed on to my generation by the feminists before us. But theory held up only until real life started, when, after years of hiking alone in the hilly walls of New York City, I began stumbling again and again through the climb of a liberated self. Where were the permanent footholds? Where was a base camp? The red stars of animals' eyes? A child? A family? Where was the blood of the land? Rumi said, "Let yourself be silently drawn by the stronger pull of what you really love." Who wouldn't agree that that's the most difficult moment of a life—not to know what you love?

Mr. Boyd, almost thirteen hundred years ago the Japanese poet Yamanoue Okura spoke of the impermanence of human life. He wrote: "We are helpless in this world. / The years and months slip past / Like a swift stream, which grasps and drags us down. / A hundred pains pursue us, one by one."

I am beginning to understand those pains as a kind of weaning from innocence, perhaps pains irrefutably necessary to understanding the freedom you spoke of all those years ago. Because your freedom wasn't an easy freedom of wind on the mountain, or sun on my face. I'm guessing now it was more of a paradoxical freedom: that of being connected to the mountain, of being bound to Sugarloaf.

It was as though you imagined someone like myself to be living in a straight line, moving forward and gaining tenacity with each inch of escape into new space; while you imagined someone like yourself living in a circle, moving round and round, grounded in the same old territory. Ultimately, though, the straight line supports much less weight and is more easily broken. It is the circle that flows in an unending stream of energy. It is the circle that offers, in its familiarity with the circle before it, another layer of strength and thus a reciprocity and interdependence. There is no authentic life, and therefore no genuine freedom, conferred outside the circle of mountain, land, and creature. The isolation of Sugarloaf, appearing to stand free itself, was a mirage. This was the teaching of our remote mountain.

And because I think it was not only the ecology of Sugarloaf Mountain you had in mind, I believe your secret freedom paralleled something of what Thoreau thought when he wrote: "I love Nature partly because she is not man, but a retreat from him. . . . If this world were all man, I could not stretch myself, I should lose all hope. He is restraint; she is freedom to me. He makes me wish for another world; she makes me content with this."

Dear Mr. Boyd, I see now—after having pursued a life of individualism, after having had a nomadic soul—that also you wished for me contentment. Thank you.

Finally, as you may have guessed, I had a child several years ago. I returned to Maryland because I believed my daughter should see the purple light of unbroken land in the morning; believed she should see hayfields swallowing deer and fox; believed she should have a community of not only people but of land and animals. Some days my child and I pass your old house on the way to visit her grandparents. She hides in the cornfields. The sun rolls down the flanks of Sugarloaf. I've taken the long way home, Mr. Boyd, but still I feel the land, our mountain, echoing in my body.

In the Slipstream

*A man's work is nothing but this slow trek to
rediscover. . . those two or three great and simple
images in whose presence his heart first opened.*
Albert Camus

One day a strong goose came into my life. She arrived at the
wildlife rehabilitation center where I was working wrapped in one
of those blankets stained with oil and the smell of gasoline and left
in the corner of car trunks for situations just like this: an injured
animal found along a road and brought in, illustrating that there
are concerned and caring individuals living in the suburbs, and that
we do get out of our cars. Still, the journey of an injured animal
is not announced with ambulance sirens. There are no families
scurrying down a clean white hall behind a doctor steeped in Ivy
League degrees. A sick or injured wild animal, unless it is a baby
with siblings or a mother with young, is catapulted into the human
world all on its own. The familiar feel of forest floor or grass, tree
bark or water under foot or paw is replaced with metal bars, wood
and wire walls, yesterday's *Washington Post,* and a heap of hope that
something can be done to save the animal's life.

When the Canada goose showed up at the rehab center, I was on
my hands and knees, buried in the cage of another goose (or gander,
it's impossible to tell the difference from feather coloration) that
eventually would be set free but was now paddling about in a
portable blue plastic pool while I cleaned its cage. The new goose
was making quite a raucous calling, and it quickly became obvious
that her personality was like that of the other geese residing at the

center: pissed-off, which is not a peculiar way for geese to be. Her fierceness, though, was of a different ilk, and for an entirely different philosophy, one might say. Her chance to bite the hand that fed her hadn't yet occurred. She hadn't done time in the metal cages or been harbored in the plastic pool that the other geese begrudgingly waddled to in the morning and refused to leave in the evening. Actually, these goose activities would have been, had she known such events existed for her captured kin, reasons for her to argue the good argument. Instead, she was here to fight the good fight, which, I believe she knew on some level, was a fight for her life: She was the goose who would not go down.

The long black velvet neck of a Canada goose is a neck designed especially for probing deep, murky waters. It is a neck that, when stretched straight during steady and tireless flights of up to sixty miles an hour over the earth, is the great identifying characteristic for those of us watching awestruck from below. It is the neck that was now swinging to and fro, side to side, an unleashed garden hose with the water turned on. The goose hissed. Her wings flapped as though she may have thought she was still flying over the fields that edge the multiplex movie theater where there is a pond in which vast numbers of Canada geese gather. Did she know that pond? Had she flown from that refuge and set down on the shoulder of a road, and been sideswiped?

Absurd as it sounds, some people go out of their way to run over suburban squirrels. And it may be the same with geese, most of which, in the urbanized East, no longer migrate and, increasingly, no longer hold a significant place in our hearts. Geese are permanent residents, having noticed the auspicious opportunities associated with suburban sprawl: vast manicured lawns of assorted business campuses; large, cleared public park lands; and an abundance of urban people, like myself, who hunger for that which is wild. Hunger, though, works both ways. What is tossed out to geese as a gesture of love—Cheerios, Pepperidge Farm Goldfish, bread crust, and empty ice-cream cones—has contributed to the drastic decline in popularity of the birds, whose inefficient diges-

in the slipstream

tive systems cause them to continuously excrete on the public
suburban grounds where they once were welcomed but are now
considered, by many, pests.

Though it once would have been a strange occurrence, it is now
commonplace to see Canada geese highway hopping as they travel
from man-made pond to man-made pond, or to see them content-
edly poking around in the purple, red, and bright orange wildflowers that grow so well, albeit so incongruously, in the grassy
median strips of multi-lane roads stitching together the suburbs of
Washington, D.C. I admit to having considered stopping in these
strangely peaceful highway strips; I have desired such surrealism
myself. Could this strong-willed goose now be thinking of flowers?

I figured it could have been otherwise. An injured and frightened bird could go down, it seemed, in the face of such struggle.
But her large and powerful heart, with the same basic design as the
human heart—one that efficiently segregates oxygenated and de-
oxygenated blood, which, for her, made all the rigors of flight possible—kept on. Other animals let go more easily. The box turtle
whose shell and body had been sliced by a lawn mower and resembled the latticed crust of cherry pie; the snake that slid into the bi-
cyclist on the road and whose body was wounded into the shape of
an exclamation point; the little brown bat—these animals went
down. Some of the creatures I fed one day would be gone the next:
the nestlings secured and sleeping in wads of toilet paper in the
heated, white, dresser-like drawers; the newborn gray squirrels—
their tiny paws kneading like a kitten's against my hand—whose
eyes never would open to the world waiting for them. Working
at the center required a uniform of sorts, a coat of toughness or a
dress of death, both of which I uncomfortably squeezed into when
necessary.

Until this goose, upon whose arrival nothing could be pinned
together, nothing fit. She landed in my life with her daring heart
that would not stop; and in so doing joined the elusive geese flying
in the open skies of my thoughts: geese in all the months of one's
life that come before, geese one senses in the months to come, geese

the hopes of snakes

in dreams, in memories, in the autumn air blanketing the corn-fields. Witnessing her struggle, I felt her grip on something that of course I could only imagine—March winds in her feathers, splash-downs in green waters, arenas of endless clover, flights under fuchsia-colored evening clouds. And it was perhaps because I believed she longed for these things, or that her heart did, that I felt a headlong rush of images of my father, whose heart, unlike hers, had, for a time, stopped.

The phone rings about a parent, a relative, a friend who has had a heart attack. It is a call that tells a literal story: This person who has inhabited your life, who has sat with you in silence, walked with you in the rain, this person with whom you've shared meals, with whom you've been to the mountains or to the ocean, this person was at some certain place, on a sunny or a cloudy day, and in the moments when you were cutting the lawn or grocery shopping, working, or studying, suddenly, or over time, even, there was pain that slowly anchored in the body, or came on violently. This pain was the heart talking, or attacking, either or both, depending on perspective. This person has survived and is in the hospital, or this person has died. Clearly, the heart has successfully besieged the body that is its home. If death has not come, questions brew about how to fix this dying heart now thought of as a weakened heart, which it literally, physically, has become but which it may always truly have been—such as a lonely heart, a sad heart, or an open heart that was too open. And so it is decided the heart must be cut, bypasses must be made, when it is possible to imagine these, in part, could be reasons the heart initially shut down: a cut and wounded heart, a bypassed heart.

The surgery is said to be routine. Papers warning of possible death are signed and soon enough the knife slices the chest. Layers of the body will be peeled back. Ribs will shine through, be bro-ken, and split apart. If such a scene could be witnessed, seemingly incompatible nightmarish images of the arched ribs of a great whale's skeleton might pass through the mind, along with the relentless ache to see the whale—its wonderful and generous and intelligent body—alive again. Wherever there is blood there is the clotting memory of moving through life with this person, this gentle whale of your life.

The hours sitting in the greenish gray waiting room tick by, and terms like *mitral valve, graft, cardiac pulsations, echocardiogram, coronary arteries, vascular system, right ventricle, angina,* and *coronary thrombosis* float in the conversations of the doctors and nurses streaming in and out of peripheral vision. Random facts from hospital FAQ sheets are remembered: a heart that beats tens of thousands of times a day; a heart like a gasoline pump, propelling blood not by cup or pint but by gallons into the tank of the body. At rare times, all of this slips into the mind and makes sense, somehow, as though it is what is known of the heart that invites us into it, rather than what is unknown.

"Ye need not go so far to seek what ye would not seek at all if it were not within you," wrote Emerson. Geese: how do they enter? Despite knowing the truth, since it could have been any suburban animal—a squirrel, a robin, a worm—it might be that geese were the first wild animals in me, my earliest glimpses occurring as a toddler standing at the edge of a suburban pond throwing breadcrumbs and French fries to these birds that, back then, truly migrated into and out of our lives. Years later, at seven, fifteen, eighteen, even at twenty-two and just before moving to Manhattan, season after season, geese were instructive in the idea of waiting. I want to say there's nothing I wouldn't do to see once more the geese in New York City. They threaded through the skyscrapers and over the Metropolitan Museum of Art, on Fifth Avenue, on their way to the reservoir in Central Park, which for the birds' arrival got all gussied up in sashes of red, orange, and yellow fall leaves. A walk through the park then was like snuggling into a gigantic autumn-colored sweater.

And what of the geese in the Arthur Kill marshlands alongside Staten Island? The ingenious pair who came upon the shore of

Prall's Island and found what could be equated with a Donald Trump–like real estate discovery: an old black car tire. It was a tire affording an open view of the Kill and, across the Kill, a dead-on view of the lime-colored New Jersey wetlands, including all the circular, white oil storage tanks that resemble the Guggenheim Museum across New York Harbor and up Fifth Avenue, near Central Park. Having fallen off one of the many trash barges passing this way, perhaps the tire could be put to good use. But first things first. Before the goose could lay her eggs, before she could imagine leading goslings through the small and dirty waves left in the wakes of oil tankers motoring by, she had to construct a nest inside the tire. So as the gander kept guard, the goose stood in the center of this tire and began gathering the necessary material within her reach: cattail leaves from the marsh, sticks, reeds, and grasses. A mere four hours later, with the nest nearly made, the goose plucked soft, satin-like feathers from her breast and padded the cup of the nest with these gifts from her body.

I wonder how, on a summer day, when the heat of a city marshland sucks all your muscles into the mud and when sweat trickles along every inch of your skin, anyone could not be tempted, as was I. Tempted, since the goslings had departed and the nest sat empty, to rest my head on this pillow of a goose nest. It's not impossible to envision beginning every day from this island, this place where a goose and gander wake to the sun over the Atlantic before flying off to Central Park, the Metropolitan, the Guggenheim. But it is unfair to claim these thoughts, these desires, these imaginings, these experiences, without mentioning my father, who, if he has not loved any certain goose, has loved something about them and has passed it on to me.

I am home from New York for a visit, and, on the December morning that I carry my crippled dog into the cornfields, I awake to the wild barking of foxhounds and random gunshots ringing through the air. A goose? A red fox? Deer? Since I was sixteen and my father moved my family thirty miles northwest, away from the denser

115

suburbs just outside of Washington, D.C., to the croplands and woodlands of Maryland's Agricultural Reserve, I have associated the sound of shotgun with the cold, with the crunching of dry leaves and the scent of chimney smoke. I didn't know then that there were hunting schedules—certain days, weeks, months for certain animals—or that the government wrote reports about the abundance of Maryland's wildlife:

> Maryland's citizens are fortunate to reside in a state that consists of a sequence of physiographic provinces that tend to bisect the region in a series of northeast/southwest swaths. Each of these regions represents interdependent physical and geographical features that influence the structure and distribution of ecological communities found within them. As a result, wildlife species and ecosystems representative of large portions of the eastern United States can be found in Maryland.

Put simply, this means there are lots of animals to hunt.

A goose is a resource, as is a piece of corn; and the harvesting of animals is executed with firearm, muzzle-loader, bow and arrow, or leghold trap. Have an urge to get out and run, chase, harass an animal? It is legal; be our guest. There are considerable choices available for those whose interests tend toward rampage and killing. Meanwhile, other citizens live with the sometimes surreptitious, yet deep, desire simply to glimpse geese, mink, river otter, coyote, opossum, raccoon, skunk, long-tailed weasel, fisher, beaver, nutria, muskrat, even bobcat.

When I arrived for this visit home, I dreamt of a reacquainting ceremony for my old, dying dog. And now, on this windy day, I will set her down in the frozen soil of brittle corn and hope she remembers her runs here and the way it was when we waited with my father for the passing of geese. It will be cold, and I am looking forward to the clear Maryland air, to the way December dives into the body, surging down the throat like so many invisible diamonds.

There have been innumerable Decembers before, when snow drew my father into the drifts to build igloos, sleigh, and play games like "fox and geese," a traditional snow country game that we called "mouse and dog." One person is dog, the hunter, and the others are mice, the hunted. Renaming the game to "mouse and dog" happened over time, as our dog—who, before she was crippled, relentlessly chased but never caught either dozens of actual mice or one very intelligent mouse—demanded her place in the moot hunt. The fun of the game was switching between one heart and another, dog into mouse, mouse into dog, and all the concealment, deception, and goofy fury that went with it, as though the animals did such things.

Even so, the sound of barking and gunshot in the air made it impossible to forget that beyond our game were actual foxes and geese; and, against my father's wishes, I remember trying to follow the sound of the gun with the falling of a goose from the sky. It was then, when I was looking for death, that my father turned me toward the birds' lives. If, as the geese hit the sky above us they were not in full V formation, my father pointed out their elegant assembling until there was nearly perfect equidistance among them all, with one goose, usually a mature gander, leading at the tip of the V. He explained the theory that when the geese trailed one another in their formation each goose encountered less air resistance and thus saved energy. It was known as flying in the slipstream, each bird's flight assisting the bird behind it, a force that drew the geese together through the sky. Though he also questioned if this sharing of energy might be thought of as one energy. Imagine, he said, watching them fly farther west, toward the green waters of the Potomac River. Eventually, the lead gander would fall out and another bird would take its place. What could that be, he asked, breaking out of his reverie, but a flock with one brilliant heart and many souls?

Still, questions of the hunt lingered. Which animal was fleeing in which province? Goose, deer, fox, mink, river otter, skunk, opossum? Unlike my game of mouse and dog, these animals did not switch between identities, did not become "other," though I've heard now that such things are said of hunting. Things like the hunted comes to inhabit the hunter, through some sense of the an-

in the slipstream

imal's compliance to surrender, or physically, later, through the eating of the animal's body—the validity of either being known only to those who've taken the shot.

Where was the hunt, and the witnesses? Some seasons, these questions were partially answered, when foxhounds, followed by men on horseback, men dressed in absurdly colorful formal jackets, stampeded through the nearly one thousand pines on our property in search of foxes clearly still alive but nonetheless running like ghosts of themselves, invisible and exquisitely fast entities attempting escape.

With all this, it should not be surprising that a dream recurs, inconsolable, as though it is a dark anthem meant to recompose the waking life, but never does. And so a goose comes again to me in the night. She falls into my dream's pale field, into the sounds of the dogs in packs, crying, yelping. A river of red spreads over her body, while the sky slowly sips away the surviving birds. I cradle the goose to my chest, autumn's yellow wind preening her. What is a goose's life but cold stories of broken ice below her body in winter and memories of warm thunderstorms punishing her flights up the wild spring water? The goose in my dream is dying beside forest fringed black with crows, dying under skies stitched with the hissing of rhapsodic vultures. I must snap the neck of this bird thrown down into these hollow hills, through which, I sense, the goose and I soon will fall. Then the season abruptly changes, and it is spring and times of light blue flying. Still, the goose is suffering on my lap. The hounds are coming, or going, when I wake up, unsure of what has happened to the goose.

After night, it is morning, and again I am convinced my father has brought me to a land of immense loss and confusion. It is my sense that I never kill the goose in my dream, though it would have been the merciful thing to do.

I remember my dream goose again when, in the one-window post office run by the Mennonite woman, I say hello to the hunters who hand me a pen while licking stamps; I think of the goose when a hunter offers up his seat to me at the ice-cream counter in town;

the hopes of snakes

the goose flashes across my mind when hunters, breaking to buy lunch, help me with groceries in the old wood-floored market too small for grocery carts. Season after season, hunters dressed in camouflage park their trucks in town. We meet face on, and I hunt for what I'm meant to say: That with them here the rest of us live in the crosshairs of cruelty? What? Something my grandmother drilled into me plays over and over: "Be kind, for everyone you meet is fighting a great battle." And so there is altogether everything and nothing in how we leave it: "Thank you."

In these wide tracts of earth absolutely drenched coral by sunset, where disappearing is possible, where if you stayed out long enough your hair smelled like wild grass, and where geese flew in slipstreams of other geese, skein after skein, my father, the dog, and I, year in year out, reckoned with the indefinite things entering our hearts.

There is a definition for a completely unpronounceable word belonging to the Yamana natives of Tierra Del Fuego, in Ushuaia, Argentina, and the definition, according to the Yamana-English dictionary printed by the Reverend Thomas Bridges in 1933 is: "to be light, not yet dark, to be a little light, light in the sky, as before day light and after sundown." It is almost like saying something is beautiful, or almost beautiful, though not ugly. Or saying something is complex, though not terribly complex, but not simple. Ideas within ideas. Contradictions. Layers upon layers. Lives within other lives. These are the things, I think now, that my father intuited could be taught me by this land, where woods met fields, where sky met earth, where new houses met old farmhouses, urban folk met rural folk, and where, while calling to geese, I met my father and began piecing together the layers of him.

In Maine in the late 1940s, the boy that would become my father lived, sporadically, in a white clapboard cottage with an outhouse, in patches of neglected soil carved out of the forest. Back then, children were less considered than today, and so uprooting, relocating, shuffling a boy between Maine and the projects of

in the slipstream

Boston and New York City, was, it seems, a normal part of the child's breaking, like a horse. Unsure of an alcoholic father's return, and existing long periods without a mother, the boy rambled through provinces of abandonment. A few faded black and white snapshots of the years in Maine reveal a boy both haunted and hunted by loss—always a slight smile, a looking away or through —as though loss can prey upon a person.

"It is a deep mystery that love is born in the mind's (and body's) experience of emptiness and loss," writes Belden C. Lane in *The Solace of Fierce Landscapes*. "The longing of the soul, made sharper by the painful absence of that which it loves . . . reaches in darkness for a beloved who comes unannounced and without guarantee."

And thus geese enter, geese as distraction, as company, as my father's beloveds, mysterious and elegant, traveling overhead on the Atlantic migratory pathway to and from their breeding grounds in Canada. And so, too, enter stray dogs and forest creatures and the birds he loved most, blue jays. I remember him telling me, when I was a child, the story of how he stalked blue jays. Their vibrant color drew him. For hours he tried outwitting them, attempting and often failing to lure the jays with suet into cages he'd fashioned out of twigs and twine. The few birds he caught he stood by, admiring them, speaking to them, feeding them. Soon, he freed them. This is how, I believe now, my father became a man made of birds and trees and why, when we moved to our field in Maryland, he planted nine hundred pines, one hundred dogwoods, and twelve pear trees, creating, essentially, a forest for himself, and for me. A forest that called in the animals—hawks, crows, mice, opossums, foxes, blue jays, robins, owls, chipmunks—the creatures that lived on the slopes of his heart, evidently long ago bypassed in childhood.

Jung said, "We are forever only more or less than we actually are," which is an idea much like the Yamana word about light— things as more finely layered and intricate than what is actually seen. I am thinking, then, of my father as a boy with blue jays, as a boy stitching together not only twigs and twine, but a torn heart, a heart lured by the wild creatures we hunt because of both our pas-

the hopes of snakes

sions and our battles. In stunningly simple yet complex moments, all those many years ago, a boy and his blue jays, or his creatures, or his geese, intermingled over and over, rising and falling, dipping in and out of what my father sensed even then was one brilliant energy —one heart with many souls. This was where, as a boy, he played: in the slipstream of animals.

And so it has come to this, to the idea of being forever only more or less than we actually are, which, in my father's understanding of the world is forever only more or less than a blue jay, or the geese migrating overhead, the geese in New York City's wastelands, or the insignificant geese in the pond by the movie theater. Of being forever the hunted fox sprinting through pines, the deer hidden in fog-covered fields; of being the strong goose who came into my life and died later that day, finally, peacefully, with her great wings folded against her like the closed petals of the flowers she loved. This is my father's legacy.

One Nation under
Coyote, Divisible

All that we are arises with our thoughts.
Buddha

Until this moment—when I am walking, quietly, through fields of long grass, vines, mud, trees, thickets, and the pale gray air of March—the day has been ordinary. Like millions of other mothers across the country, I sent my child off to school, accomplished some work, and ran errands. Now, not far beyond the field I am in, rush hour is winding down, stoves warm dinner, families relax inside their homes—in the country, the suburbs, the city—where the nightly news lights up dens along the East Coast. Parents kiss and play with giggling children they've missed all day. The family dog or cat scratches repeatedly at the door, asking to be let out into the peach-lit sky and then to come in, again and again. But just as the news ends and the dishes are cleaned, things will change. For outside, beyond the dens of humans, in the scattered winds of owls and near gatherings of wild geese, is the eastern coyote, the coyote stretching into the evening and, I hope, into the slowly darkening moments ahead.

Walking beside me is Rob Gibbs, a wildlife ecologist with the Montgomery County Park Department in Maryland, where, on the outskirts of Washington, D.C., sightings of coyotes have increased over the past few years. Behind us is my husband, who, during our half-hour drive from D.C., described how his boss, in Manhattan, where we lived for many years, believes our excursion to find coyotes is not all that impressive. This man's disinterest, or lack of enthusiasm, is due to the fact that he lives in Westchester County, New York, an affluent suburb outside Manhattan that since I left has been infiltrated by coyotes that, it is said, wound their way down from the Adirondacks. As my husband spoke about his boss, I remembered once again the coyote that ventured out of Westchester through Yonkers and then headed south into the densely populated borough of the Bronx, from whence it had to cross the Harlem River, by swimming or by bridge, to arrive on the agonizingly populated shore of Manhattan. Naturalists theorize that, once in Manhattan, the coyote made its way south through Riverside Park and then scratched its way east along the streets of the Upper West Side to arrive, finally, in a landscape the coyote surely believed was, at the very least, some approximate rendition of wilderness: Central Park. But before long, on April Fool's Day 1999, the thirty-five-pound coyote was stalked by urban park rangers and hit with a tranquilizer dart a few blocks from the famous Plaza Hotel on the park's southern edge. This occurred not long after I arrived in Washington; and ever since I have wondered, How did I leave New York, travel through gray walls, south, when coyotes were coming closer toward my life, from the north?

This does not mean coyotes were not already in Maryland, because they were, out in the fringes, in the foothills west toward West Virginia. But just as water dripping from a faucet grows into an overflowing puddle, so too has the coyote population grown, and begun to stream east through the state. The fact is that right now Maryland has the fine distinction of being, along with Delaware, the state in which coyotes from the north and coyotes from the south are converging. So it seems, after all, that I have arrived in just the right place at the right time. As Rob, my husband and I move on, I picture in my head a map of the United States and imagine upon it two shaggy arrows of gray and reddish brown fur, one curving down the East Coast, one curving up, until, in Maryland, the arrowheads meet along the Potomac River, virtually on the doorstep of the President of the United States, where in the nearby

one   nation   under   coyote,   divisible

123

woods of dusk and dawn, the country's foremost canine predator is forming a new native American nation: the Nation of Eastern Coyote.

One way to find a coyote, Rob has told us already, is to search deeper into McKee-Beshers Wildlife Management Area, the official name of this brushy, thicketed, wooded, and swampy landscape along the Potomac River that is one of the wildest spots in all the state, though it is only thirty or so minutes outside of Washington, D.C. As the sun drops closer to the horizon, Rob will set on the ground a tape-recorded "predator call," which will play the voice of an animal in distress. Tonight, the distress will be that of a rabbit, since coyotes enjoy eating rabbits. Coyotes also are one of the best mouse catchers working today; and when rabbits and mice are unavailable, moles and voles are preferred. The curious and smart coyote, which is all coyotes, will, we hope, awaken to its nocturnal day and—eagerly anticipating dinner or, depending on how one twists time, breakfast—come investigate the call of the distressed rabbit. We will wait, crouched down, our backs against brush and trees, behind rabbit's crying, and downwind of what I imagine will be fields of emerging coyotes.

I have, in my life, glimpsed the silhouette of a coyote, once. It was two years ago, and it occurred so fast that had I been tuning the car radio or glancing left instead of right, I could not be claiming to have seen what I believe I saw. In fact, my conclusion that the animal actually was a coyote has come to me with increased confidence only recently, which often leaves me to tell a still somewhat hesitant-sounding story, depending on who is listening. After all, a coyote is something like a UFO in these parts: some people believe in them, some don't; and so you make midcourse adjustments as you speak, knowing instinctively who is which, or, at least, who desires to believe in the mysterious.

There are not many more facts to tell, except that I was driving down a well-traveled, yet dark, two-lane road at 10:15 P.M., just three minutes beyond the city limits of Washington, into Maryland, when not far from one of the sporadically lit street lamps there stood, like a shadow, like a ghost, a German-shepherdish creature. Though in the split second that my mind registered *dog,* I also questioned what was no longer visible: *the legs were too long, the body was too thin, it disappeared too quickly.*

It is useful to know, however, that at the time of my questionable coyote sighting I had recently had a baby. A related thought is that I wasn't out much at night back then, and so, when by chance I did get out, I was operating in that depleted state of exhaustion known as the constantly-nursing-baby-syndrome. Women in this realm drown fast in what we mothers call "mother muddle." Muddle is forgetting words midsentence, phone numbers as you are dialing them, and many other ordinary, common things that previously kept us on track and believing we lived in the human world. Positively identifying, while in muddle, an animal on the side of the road, in the dark, in, virtually, the city, as a coyote? *Nah.*

But it kept at me, this coyote. When I took my infant daughter down to the Potomac River's muddy paths in her SUV-like stroller, I looked for coyote tracks. If it was not spring and the time of coyote birth, when coyotes spend their days by the den in a side of a hill, there was a chance a coyote would have settled near rock piles, in a hollow log, under ledges, in a drainage pipe, of which there are several along the river, or in the woodsy and grassy sides of the path. For some reason, perhaps because I myself was sleep-deprived, I fantasized about finding coyote's bed. Locating the private place of a coyote, where it dreamed and secretly cycled through the same stages of sleep as I once had, held an inexplicable allure. Though I never deluded myself with the idea that what I'd just heard was a group of howling coyotes, sometimes I stopped the stroller fast, thinking, mistakenly it would turn out, that what was a bird or a squirrel had been a coyote's yelp or yip. By the end of our walks, I'd pointed out to my baby the red-eared sliders sunning in the water, the whitewash of owls, a great blue heron or two, seagulls, kingfishers. No coyote.

Until eight months later when, in my mothers' group one Fri-

one   nation   under   coyote,   divisible

day morning, wherein seven or so mothers—and their plump, rosy-cheeked, crawling babies—came to my house for banana bread and coffee. It was then, between bouts of babies crying, that one of the mothers brought up an article about coyotes that she had read in the local weekly paper. This news ended any discussions about weaning babies, disciplining kids, sex, or the lack of it.

In one moment, the mere mention of a word—coyote—changed everyone. Some of the excitement dangling in the air was leavened with protective instincts and with fear of a foreign creature, a predator, in our suburban midst. Though I wondered, too, how much each woman inherently understood how close the perceived personality of a coyote matched her own psyche as a mother. For what is a mother in the modern world if not—as she juggles children and work and life—a coyote: a spontaneous creature by necessity; a creature defying fixed roles; one who, like the coyote, looks for shortcuts and realizes the essential health of playfulness over seriousness.

Whatever each of us individually and silently thought, it was clear that for this morning at least nothing was more important in the world than coyotes. A new story had arrived in the lives of these women; and it was about not only the birth of their awareness of the coyote, but about the real wild animal, itself. This was when I began thinking of the presence of the coyote as something of a request. A request that we create our own new Eastern stories, different from the Western ones, for this predator, stories which necessarily might begin with: Coyotes, what could they mean to me?

My sister lives in Virginia's horse country, where she keeps her horses and the stray dogs she has rescued. On her large landscape of fields and woods, live owls, foxes, crows, hawks, snakes, fence lizards, and, one day she dreams, coyotes. Every so often she calls to let me know she heard something in the night, although what, exactly, she is unsure. A man who lives nearby my sister, a man who talks to horses and whose horses listen, says that for several years now he has seen coyotes, up on the dusty gravel road leading to his ranch, at twilight. Without much hesitation, he thinks he may shoot one. Once, when this man handed me a beer and welcomed me into his home, he detailed the sordid story of the stuffed raven I noticed sitting on his coffee table, the raven he'd shot long ago, when only small pockets of the birds still flew east of the Mississippi. Another man declared recently that if he had sheep and a sheep was killed, he would blame coyotes, and shoot one. He doesn't have sheep so perhaps he's joking, but it's hard to tell, especially since the idea of killing is spoken with such ease, while smiling.

I want to say to those willing to shoot at the unknown—to shoot at what is perceived as a threat—that perhaps certain explicit information would calm their fears. For instance, coyote's main diet is not sheep but rabbits, mice, voles, moles, woodchucks, fruit, corn, and carrion. A coyote's overall temperament and behavior are not vicious; it will not attack, in packs, the lone person out for a walk; and it has been known, when captured, to roll belly-up, like a dog. Coyotes can be affectionate and sociable, or solitary and seemingly lonely. Some coyotes mate for life, and the male, female, and their offspring constitute the "pack." Pups from this pack may, instead of venturing out on their own, stay on for a while with their parents to help raise babies born in the following year.

Knowledge—does it make it any easier to redirect one's rage?

In the complicated Eastern landscapes where humans mix with coyote, it is helpful to remember Emerson, who said: "You shall have joy, or you shall have power . . . you shall not have both." In the end, I wander south to my sister's land in Virginia because her open fields nip at me, reminding me of the agricultural landscape where we spent the later years of our childhood, and where my sister, on one of her walks, found Brandy, a wounded but sonsy wild husky that so resembled a wolf we believed she had brought one home.

Sonsy, which means attractive and healthy, comes from the Irish Gaelic *sonas,* which means "good fortune." Brandy brought good fortune, if it can be considered as something other than wealth, as something that instead brings one a sense of living authentically. For some months before we found her, Brandy had lived outside, in woods, in wind. She drank from the little brown-water creek. She slept curled in a perfect circle, her head wrapped around her legs and her tail over her nose. She brought to us the earth that had settled in her, the earth's ease with silence, the earth's ease with solitude; and though after she healed and could've run, she stayed. Afternoons, we followed her through sun or rain as she trotted, nose up in air, then down to soil, hoping to catch a mouse's scent or movement. When day turned and the sky's upper edges darkened, Brandy sat by the sliding glass door, looked into the world with her eyes of crystal blue light, and howled, singing of something eternal that, when she was free like a wolf, or like a coyote, had inhabited her, inhabited her still, and over time came to inhabit us so much that we would run our hands over her thick furred back, rub our cheeks on her snout, and beg, "Brandy...howl, girl." We wanted to be taken. We wanted accompaniment, as though Brandy's howling was a song, a ballad, a peaceful greeting to the unknowns of the dark night ahead.

My old coyote-silhouette story came to mind when I first called to ask Rob to take me on what could be called a predator search, since a variety of predators other than coyotes—owls, for instance, or foxes—might appear. But I wasn't shy; I had a lust for coyote. The silhouette—it had just not been enough. Seeing a coyote for longer than a moment was, to be honest, an experience I felt I deserved. A need, really, the origins of which, it is my hunch, had grown from the attempts we all make to understand the misunderstood creatures in one's life, whether they be people or animals.

My desire cut deep into that vein of longing that stretches between a person and, say, the cosmos. Things you think you never will have and keep asking for, silently, anyway. For everyone, there is always something, isn't there? In our private moments an almost childlike urgency: an "I wish, I wish upon a star...to see a coyote, near or far." I will admit—if one can talk about karma or a sense of justness the universe deals—how, two years after I'd seen the coyote silhouette and when by that time newspapers were running a coyote article here and there, I increasingly felt it unfair that people who perhaps never wanted to see a coyote, who had not wished upon any stars, nonetheless had been visited by a coyote. In the garage, reported one local newspaper. Eating a squirrel in the front yard, described another. Or the veterinarian who in the *Washington Post* cited the story of his client, a farmer who had had his "barn swept clean of nearly ten barn cats by coyotes."

Then, too, there had been those who had not seen but heard coyote and described the coyote howl as "haunting," reported the *Post,* as "very chilling," "troubling," and "creepy," reminding me of what Jung said: We are "afraid of anything new because it contains unknown powers, indefinite dangers.... Everybody is afraid, nobody likes new ideas; they always throw people into a panic, and where there is panic, there is bloodshed."

Bloodshed is the predominant American story of the western coyote, as well as its cousin and old foe, the wolf—the predator our twenty-sixth president, Theodore Roosevelt (for whom the teddy bear is named, with reference to his bear hunting) called "the archetype of ravin, the beast of waste and desolation." Early Americans came to the shores of this country with an inherited European hatred for the wolf, which grew vehemently to include the coyote. Although I'm an easterner, I don't think I'd be remiss if I said that many westerners think of the coyote (or "Song Dog," "God's Dog," or "Little Wolf") as a symbol of all that is wild and free, but that some consider the coyote, who like the wolf has at times been known to prey on goats, chickens, and lambs, an eliminable nuisance. Through what is currently and euphemistically called Wildlife Services (WS), and what for many decades was more realistically termed Animal Damage Control (ADC), the United States government has, since the early 1900s, destroyed the millions of coyotes, wolves, mountain lions, and bears that ranchers condemn as livestock-killers. This service costs the American people ten million taxpayer dollars per year, and it continues to this day despite a U.S. Government Accounting Office report issued fifteen years ago that found ADC kills coyotes even when damage to livestock has not occurred.

Surprising as it sounds, as early as 1906 the renowned nature writer John Burroughs claimed that the predators in Yellowstone "certainly needed killing," a comment likely directed at wolves, "the quintessential predator," writes Lisa Mighetto in *Wild Animals and American Environmental Ethics*. Though by now the majority of Americans understand wolves as shy, reclusive animals that are not a threat to humans, Mighetto says, "the *idea* of the wolf... has been more terrifying than the behavior of the actual animal." Coyote, being such a close cousin to wolf, suffers from the same antipathy. "Throughout the twentieth century coyotes in this country have suffered numerous atrocities," writes Mighetto, "including being ignited alive and left to starve with their mouths wired shut; some have even been scalped."

Over the last twenty-five years, WS/ADC has destroyed seventy-five thousand to ninety thousand coyotes *per year* in, mostly, seventeen Western states. This management tactic successfully accomplishes two things. First, it elevates the risk of an overabundance of the rodents and other small mammals coyotes are so important in controlling. Look, for example, at an old black and white photograph courtesy of the Idaho State Historical Society, Boise. Published in Mighetto's book, it depicts five men, a few of them in suits, standing by a large cart drawn by two horses standing on a wet, muddy or snowy, road. The year is 1912. It is daylight, morning perhaps, and each man is holding, upside down and by one leg, a dead jackrabbit. In the cart, piled high and sliding off of one another's furry torsos, are the bodies of the other 1,195 jackrabbits the men had shot, "representing one night's catch," reads the photo's caption. One night.

Second, killing coyotes simply makes more of them. When coyotes inhabit a landscape where hunting is not allowed, such as modern-day Yellowstone, they live in social groups in which, for the most part, only the dominant pair breeds; others in the group, the younger, less dominant individuals, are, essentially, behaviorally sterile. Lift this arrangement out of Yellowstone, though, and set it down in an unprotected landscape of relentless persecution, where virtually all coyote social groups have been dismantled, and the logical outcome is that, without dominant pairs, breeding is acceptable for all.

That the behavioral ecology of the coyote—arguably the most adaptable, successful, and incredibly intelligent midsize predator roaming this country today—is, somehow, overlooked, allows WS/ADC to continue its mission. In addition to the aerial gunning (which is shooting from a helicopter) of coyotes and other predators, additional methods of sanitizing the landscape—poisons, gasses, snares, and leghold traps—consequently destroy many "nontarget" animals: dogs, opossums, foxes, skunks, vultures, badgers, and raccoons, to name several.

This is in sharp contrast to the Native American relationship to the coyote, an animal understood and admired for its intelligence, cunning, and joyful spirit. Navajo stories, for instance, served— says a gem of an old Interior Department booklet entitled *Coyote Tales,* published in 1949—"to instruct the young with regard to right and wrong, and many times the characters [were] personified animals.... A story might illustrate the fact that the strong should not use their strength to take things from the weak." There are stories like "Coyote and Rabbit," wherein coyote is "out-coyoted," so to speak, by rabbit, coyote's main food. We have "Coyote and Crow," in which coyote's mischievous and sneaky behavior leads to his own demise as he chomps down on a cactus instead of the yummy bluebird dinner crow had led coyote to believe was waiting under a hat. And we have "Coyote and the Fawn's Stars," in which a seemingly sweet deer mother resorts to tricking a gullible coyote father. In the story, coyote admires the spots, or stars, on the backs of deer's fawns and expresses a desire that his babies be adorned with stars. Deer appears quite civilized and helpful during the encounter, and she manages the situation thus: "When my babies are very little, I build a big fire. The sparks from the fire make the stars. You can do that for your babies," she directs coyote. "Then they will have pretty stars, too." Coyote misunderstands deer and puts its babies straight into the fire. Deer watches, knowing this is wrong, but she does not prevent it. When coyote asks, "Have they been in the fire long enough? Will they have pretty stars now?" Deer says, "Yes," and she runs away laughing, knowing that all the young coyotes have died. Coyote was angry, the story continues, and so chased deer, and "still chases deer, but he never catches her."

Is "Coyote and the Fawn's Stars" meant to inspire belief in one's own beauty? Is it about revenge, since it is, after all, the weaker of the two personalities who has in the past had her beloveds killed by the stronger? Is it simply an attempt to explain why coyotes ever began chasing deer in the first place? Or might the meaning reside in something else altogether?

"Everyone is a moon," wrote Mark Twain, "and has a dark side," like the deer, "which he never shows to anybody." Except perhaps when it comes to coyotes. Then the moon may, at times, shine brightly with the fear, aggression, and loathing reserved for predators. As civilized as our nation is, coyotes make it clear that there is a wildness running through our landscapes, and, evidently, through ourselves: Could it be we need to manage our own wildness more than that of the coyote's? Or could we say of coyotes what the poet Tanaka Shozo said of rivers: "The care of rivers is not a question of rivers, but of the human heart"?

In the way that "love, like death, changes everything," wrote the mystic Kahlil Gibran, so too does hate change everything. And it is within this emotional aversion that the story of the eastern coyote began. Imagine it if you will, the Northeast woods of the United States in the early part of the twentieth century, when the few remaining wolves—those rare descendants of wolves that had escaped Roosevelt's and Burroughs's wrath and that outlasted nearly three hundred years of American abhorrence, three hundred years of being shot on sight—still roamed these deepest and most impenetrable places. With all other forests in the United States clean of wolves, western coyotes took to walking, as they will. And so somewhere back then, a coyote arrived in the Northeast woods on, say, a March evening in the bitter cold hills of Maine or Vermont and ran into a wolf, a wolf long alone without its pack.

The two canines met. They sniffed and, one would have to guess, came to some sort of an agreement about their chance evening meeting. Who knows how long they ran together; if they shared prey; if they played, as we know they do; if they howled, on the same nights, together, their own distinct howls. We have no human witnesses and are therefore, some sixty to eighty years later, left with a mystery of cold nights, dark trees, winds, moonlight, and two canine species making themselves anew. If it sounds like a romance, maybe it was. If it sounds like two creatures driven by re-lated biology, hormones, and instincts, maybe it was that as well. This is how the world evolves. As the Upanishads said, it is a time of being lead "from the unreal to the real." It is mysteriousness moving into our lives like love—unrestrained and stormy, but gripping, until finally there is surrender, an acceptance of it all as a gift, a present that each day will unwrap itself before us.

What is known, however, is that not long after this time the wolf permanently left the upper reaches of the northeastern United States and retreated into the Canadian wilderness, while the coyote, imbued with wolf's genes, grew bigger than its western predecessor and trickled slowly into the rapidly developing East Coast.

Rob was patient when, earlier, as we were walking into McKee-Beshers, I thought I'd found a coyote track in the mud, which, I ab-solutely was convinced, looked like the picture of one I'd etched into my mind, the one with the defining claws on toes three and four, the center toes. "Paw size is perfect," Rob agreed as he bent down closer to take a look, "but could just as well have been a dog's," he concluded, as he tipped down the visor of his olive green baseball cap and rose to continue walking. Rob is wearing what he suggested I wear, greens and browns, camouflage-colored cotton clothing that, unlike synthetic clothing, does not, under your arms or between your thighs, annoyingly *swish, swish, swish*—the noise of humans easily detected by coyote. In the short time we have been in the beige fields, I have watched Rob, who is cautious, like an animal. He senses when to stop; he spots things in the brush I would not see; he cups his hand to his ears and makes them more canid-like to funnel sounds of the fields into himself—a scratchiness to his left, the tousled grass to the right. He appears to notice, at once, the ground and the sky—pointing out a sharp-shinned hawk one moment and whispering, "deer, in the corner, there" the next. The land we walk through is state hunting land, and so here there are only a mere twelve white-tailed deer per square mile, compared to the county's more densely overpopulated parks and suburban landscapes, where one hundred to two hundred deer live per square mile. Rob spends his days attempting to find solutions that would control the county's explosive deer population, and he hopes that, somehow, the growing number of coyotes might help thin the herds. There are no figures, though, for the population of eastern coyotes living in the area. We know only that they are here, that whatever their numbers might be it is estimated those numbers could be growing by 15 to 25 percent a year, and that, as Rob says, coyotes are viewed by more than a few in the area as "wolves in miniature," that is, as adversaries.

Spring peepers crank up the volume of their peeping as, thirty minutes into our coyote search, which is a long time of our intermittent rabbit's crying, the upper portions of the pale gray sky have turned a truer purplish blue. An endless stream of jets blaze toward the airports—Reagan National and Dulles International—not all that far from us. We are downwind and smell what the light breezes shed our way: pools of mud, dry, late-winter grass, cool, evening air, dead leaves. Ducks fly low over the darkening fields, and head north. They must hear our injured rabbit below them; and at the moment they are overhead I watch their wings, trying to confirm my suspicion that the calls of the rabbit motivate them to fly faster.

I believe that certain things matter to animals; and though it's just a guess, it seems that the squealing, unrelenting sound of a rabbit's pain would be one of those things. We are starting to feel that our using this sound to out-trick the biggest trickster—a live, frolicking coyote—might prove us fools.

My knees are aching from the poses of stillness I am attempting to hold—rock, or tree stump, though I haven't the strength of either. Waiting for coyotes even in a place Rob guesses is prime coyote habitat will be, it appears, an enterprise of patience, hope, and exceedingly good luck. I distract myself by replaying in my mind the easy-to-come-by textbook facts about the coyote, an animal that is, one could say, through and through a true blue-blooded American, being that coyotes are native only to North America. Coyote is a fast runner, clocking up to forty miles an hour, which makes it the fastest of all North American canids patrolling its territory of anywhere from one to ten square miles. If it lives past adolescence, which 50 percent of coyotes do not, the animal I wish to see tonight could be eight to twelve years old, its lifespan in the wild. Coyote is a capable swimmer and an agile jumper, both of which give it an advantage over bobcats when hunting rabbits that, nimble and fast themselves, have been known to dive into water to escape—behavior that deters the feline, but not the canine. Including its bushy, black-tipped, foot-long tail, a coyote's grayish, reddish, brownish body is about four feet long; shoulder height is about two feet; and the eastern coyote, who is larger than its western counterpart, weighs, generally, anywhere from twenty to more than fifty pounds. This identifying information is something to grab onto, I think, as I squint through the binoculars, waiting for the fiery figure of a coyote that might match the sizes and colors I have in my head. Still, all of these facts are not unlike my saying I am five feet, eight inches tall; weigh 130 pounds; that I have brownish, reddish, grayish, longish hair; and that my home range is about ten square miles east, north, and south from my den at Little Falls along the Potomac River. Certain facts provide certain knowledge. But what are our joys and privacies? What shapes our dreams; what have we lost; what do we desire? What, when night falls, would be the stories we would tell to those waiting to listen?

Though she died years ago, I keep looking for Brandy, for the movements of her wolf-like, coyote-like body in what has now become a moonlit field, dark except for the occasional passing of a red-tinted light Rob shines into the long grass and brushy trees. We search for the yellow eyes of coyotes that we hope are venturing toward our tape-recorded sounds and thus toward the question coyote carries in its own mind: *Rabbit? Dying rabbit?* If a coyote dares, Rob says, it will circle, like all great predators, and then dash, run, dart toward us, figuring *a rabbit in distress is being distressed by another animal—an animal*, thinks coyote, *that may itself be edible, if I can get to it fast enough.* Behavior not much different than my hurrying to the two-for-the-price-of-one sale at Sears. Or, in coyote's—and McDonald's—reasoning: Eat one, get one free! This is coyote cleverness. Coyote consciousness.

A predator search being what it is, it does not include an actual incident of predation. I will not see the superb thinking skills of a coyote. Will not see coyote ally itself with badger, as one of the old myths has it. Will not see badger (who does not live in these parts anyway) do all the hard work of digging up rodent from its burrow only to have coyote waiting at the other end of rodent's underground tunnel where, when rodent pops up to escape badger, coyote grabs it. Will not see a patient coyote sitting on a frozen lake by the hole of an otter fishing below the ice. Will not see the industrious otter poke its cool, wet head up through its icy hole and slap down its sparkling fish, at which time coyote will steal it instantly. Will not see coyote chasing a larger animal in circles, as it might a pronghorn antelope on the open plains of the West, until coyote tires and gestures, somehow, to a buddy coyote to take over the chase, continuing until the antelope succumbs, whereupon the companions will divvy up dinner. Will not see coyote glancing to-

the hopes of snakes

ward the daylit sky for the flight of crows or vultures, a hint of the carrion below on the ground.

Truth is, might not see anything at all out here. We have, after almost an hour, milked this first spot, Rob says. It is time to move on, especially before our poor old rabbit tape, and our knees, die out. We discuss heading further into the countryside, toward a place called Poolesville, where reports of coyotes have been more numerous. Part of me wants to stay where we are, along the river, since I imagine that coyotes living here could be those that at night travel safely and secretly down the densely wooded, dark, and remote towpath of the C&O Canal, which borders the Potomac on the Maryland side of the river, and would lead a coyote, should a coyote decide to make the trip, right to my stone cottage overlooking the river. My sense is that my silhouette-coyote, who disappeared into the woods, lives here in McKee-Beshers.

Another part of me thinks Poolesville is a better bet, not necessarily because of previous reports about coyotes, which to anyone else might be the more significant and rational reason to head out there, but, instead, because of an old and unusable sterling silver fountain pen that in the 1800s belonged to Hettie M. Poole, daughter of Mr. Poole, founder of Poolesville, and which, on Christmas day 1982, came to belong to me. There is a story of this pen, a spirit in it that, whenever I fail to attend to the mysteries of the nonhuman world—whenever, for instance, I walk without listening for sopranos in the trees, or fail to turn my head toward the cries of crows; whenever I dismiss the smell of rain and fire on a cold day, or do not smile at angry squirrels; when I neglect noticing the blood of road-killed snakes and deer as the blood of sentient beings —then the story of my pen reminds me that it is not always the human world which shows us the way.

That Christmas day in 1982, when I was twenty, the man who is now my husband handed me his gift. I unwrapped an old, polished, smallish wooden box that once had belonged to his grandmother, and in which she had kept her precious silver belongings.

He had lined the box with golden silk and had fashioned, on the inside edge, a ledge. Upon this ledge, cocooned in yet more silk, was a fountain pen like none I had seen, a pen carved dense with flowers and intricate vines, except for a smooth, plain space of oval on the silver, in which were the engraved initials *H. M. P.*—Hettie M. Poole. Immediately, I was told the history of this woman, told of the old wooden store in which the pen had been found, and told that, alas, the pen did not work. We would need to fix it. And so I ran my fingers along the flowers and vines, as though they were braille for the natural world I so loved.

But you know Christmas day, or any important religious holiday, and how, when there are no children present or yet born to the family, there is abundant time to eat and talk, and when, after dinner when it is quiet, you return to the living room to gaze at gifts exchanged, or to look out the window, or stare at the fire. This was when, as everyone left the chandeliered dining room and headed toward the brightly lit Christmas tree in the living room, that I once again took out my pen. We passed it around the eight people present until someone suggested I try it. Maybe the salesperson had been wrong, maybe the pen, if dipped in ink, would actually work.

I opened a bottle of black ink, dipped the pen in, scraped the excess ink off on the edge of the bottle and, just as the tip of the pen touched the paper, all the lights in the house immediately, magically, frightfully went out. The people who would one day become my in-laws, the men who would become my brothers, and their girlfriends—all of us sat suddenly decorated in darkness. It was a mystery that seemed solvable, simple enough—*Here I am, folks, Hettie M. Poole. Don't even think of using my pen!*

But was that it?

In the years since, I have come to understand the mystery wasn't about death, about Hettie's death, but about birth: the birth of a new awareness on a night that was otherwise meant as a celebration of newness, acceptance, and miracles. It was Christmas night, the night we'd been taken under the wing of a presence that, as I think of it now, was much like the presence of animals in our lives: For does not the inaccessibility to an animal's mind and thoughts throw us into some state of darkness? A wild animal—I cannot ask anything of it. Instead, animals sprint across the backlit stages of our thoughts, or in the literal darkness of our streets. We cannot ask what is an animal's experience of generosity and devotion, of suffering, of nourishment and exile, what it is for them to have possibilities, to know terror and love, to understand possession, to bid farewell, feel awe, to know loneliness and gratitude, starlessness, sorrow, and loss. But "the difficulty or even the impossibility, of conveying to others the exact nature of something," writes Donald Griffin in *Animal Minds,* "does not rule it out of existence or deprive it of significance."

It seems, then, that the mystery of Hettie, of what she birthed into our lives that night, was an awareness of paradox: That it is perhaps in not always asking for verification that we come to know in our hearts something is true.

Eventually, at the requests of those with me, I lifted the pen, whereupon all the colorful lights miraculously fluttered back on. Many Christmases have since passed. I never did have the pen fixed, and have never since put it to paper. I prefer simply to remember Hettie, who all those years ago embroidered mystery into my days, who crossed into light and then took it away to reveal that, even in the darkness of night, there is a world more decorated, ornamented, and interwoven than we may know. This was why, when Rob suggested we head to Poolesville, I thought it might be Hettie, or the paradox of Hettie that, more than anything else, would now lead us into vines of coyotes.

With the decision made about Poolesville, Rob asks if we can first make a stop along a road that cuts through fields of the nocturnal woodcock's "singing grounds," fields in which songs of foreplay, songs meant to attract woodcock hens, are sung. The fields become mating grounds from February to May, and then, some three weeks later, transform into birthing grounds. Depending on whom you ask, a woodcock is also known as a timberdoodle, a big-eye, a bog-sucker, or a mudbat—not the most attractive-sounding names, especially since the male woodcock is something of a romantic.

It will be good, though, to listen for a while to romance rather than to death, to listen for, as Rob describes it, the buzzing *peeent* sound of the male woodcock. Rob *peeent*s the sound himself and explains that this is the song of the male while he is on the ground. After the woodcock's *peeent,* the bird takes off into the night sky, his wings composing a musical whistle as he ascends two or three hundred feet in the air. In the dark, he circles randomly with what guidebooks describe as a "bubbly chipping," before he descends, spiraling and zigzagging his way back to earth, back to his grassy field, singing his liquid and warbling *pee chuck tee chuck chip chip chip*.

And so it is this love song we are after—as though we are hens listening for the most beautiful boy in the grass—when we pull over and idle Rob's truck on the side of a lonely two-lane road within the territory of McKee-Beshers's black fields of grass, woods, and thickets, and under a moon still rising, which means it is still more dark than it is light. This is when, quite unexpectedly, when we have not asked, when we have not positioned ourselves downwind on our miserable old knees for hours, begging with a taped rabbit call, that we hear not a *peeent* but what I am only able to describe as a hurt woman, a woman screaming from the bottom of her belly. She screams again, a primal, bone-chilling scream, from our left, in the darkness. Rob shuts off the truck. Another scream. We open our doors—another scream—step into the road, and barely close the doors, hoping not to frighten away whatever animal is out there, calling. That I am describing to myself the sound of this animal as an injured, dying woman is, I feel, so unfair and unforgivable that I dare not mention it to Rob or my husband. I stand in the dark thinking what a sucker I am, so capable of being influenced by newspaper reports that I cannot hear beyond the fear-ridden descriptions of how others have described the coyote's howl: *bone-chilling, haunting, eerie.* This is not what I care to believe from anyone, most of all myself.

I remember then—as I stand against the truck waiting for Rob to pull out his tape-recorded rabbit and a tape-recorded coyote howl that he thinks might cause the creature in the field to call back—I remember, then, that a coyote's voice should sound higher pitched than a wolf's voice, which, thanks to Brandy, is a voice I know well, a lower, more monotone moaning. Rob is not quick to conclude anything. As he sets up the predator calls, there is a commotion of wild geese in what I can just barely make out as scattered clumps of brush and trees in the darkness. Wings flap riotously, chaotically; and in the blackness my body begins to feel what I cannot see, which is the uneasy and breaking feeling of dense feathers smashing up against feathers. There are geese honking, yelling, and then, stillness, nothing, as though I am not only blind, but now have gone deaf.

The woman in the field stops screaming.

Rob whispers in my ear that a coyote howls to be heard by another coyote. That is, they don't howl for nothing. Aside from revealing where each might be in the grass or woods, a howl also sends out information, the precise nature of which is privy to only coyotes but that may signal to a mate that prey has been located. A sort of *come on, honey, dinner's done!*

Rob plays the recorded version of a coyote; and, in its beginnings at least, it is a voice quite different from the screaming woman I have just heard. There are doggish-sounding barks, yips, and yaps; and as I listen to them they remind me of the small talk of a husband when a wife wants deeper conversation. But then the recorded coyote breaks into a prolonged, wailful howl that, as the howl ascends toward its ending, sounds like a woman, like the woman in our field, in its tremulous, shivering way. The creature now silent in the darkness may be—Rob is beginning to concede—a coyote, a coyote that had essentially cut to the chase and moved right into the deep conversation. And I think: *well this is just like a woman!*

Rob wants to be sure this is a coyote. But because we are not downwind of the animal, we will have, Rob says, immense difficulty convincing the creature to come any closer, or even to head in

one   nation   under   coyote,   divisible

the direction of our smelly humanness. Rob switches to the rabbit tape. Earlier in the night we were downwind and behind the rabbit's calling, which meant that any possible coyotes would have had to rely on and respond to their sense of hearing and sight, for the most part. Now, we are sending out mixed messages to the coyote: a rabbit's calling with a human smell; indeed, we are making everything seem fishy.

Nonetheless, Rob, who himself has never seen a coyote, is determined. Which is helpful because, as he lifts the red-tinted light into our field of silence, we see through our binoculars that there are two round yellow eyes moving east and west, then a bit north toward us, and back south, then east again, and west. The use of the red light from where we are, about sixty yards away, allows us only to see eyes and only works, of course, if the animal happens to be glancing our way. Bodies cannot be discerned at this distance until the light is replaced with a white light, which immediately startles animals into bolting away. Rob has seen the night eyes of fox; and these, he believes, are the eyes of coyote—larger, more widely spaced, higher off the ground. Through watching the animal's eyes we watch a coyote move across the field like a tennis player—up to the net, then back, across the court one way and then the other. It is clear that decisions are being made: coyote thinking, desiring; coyote responding to joy and sizing up the situation: *What are the possibilities of this rabbit? When is the time to run? What might be my loss?*

As this is going on, four sets of golden eyes, not all that far from the coyote, begin floating toward us. The eight golden eyes are like the distant lights of a ship in a calm night sea. Even higher from the ground than those of the tennis player, the lights are coming at us more deliberately and slowly until, with one glance back to see how the tennis player is faring, the ship's lights disperse and disappear into the ocean of McKee-Beshers. I search again for them—the eyes of four white-tailed deer—but it is as though they were never here.

A barred owl hoots; we turn to the sound; and the owl bears down across the brown sky behind us to perch in a dead tree. No woodcocks are *peeent*ing. No howling, no screaming woman. Occasionally, a speeding country truck roars by, rattling down the main road. Breezes of wild grass, cool winter air, and far-off chimney smoke linger around us. The time has now come simply to be with the bright yellow eyes of an otherwise invisible coyote, the yellow eyes of the new story we will tell, the story of the eastern coyote as the sunshine of the night.

Talks with Vultures

You must proceed there, that way,
where today you are least at home.
Friedrich Nietzsche

The first thing you should know about Mattie Libre is that her surname, Libre, means, in French, "free." Libre is not Mattie's birth or married name; in fact, Mattie's grown daughter suggested Libre as an appropriate moniker for her mother after Mattie divorced her first husband, who was convicted in the early 1990s for crimes of extortion against the U.S. government. Thus, the name Libre took on a somewhat double meaning. That is, Mattie was now free from a man who had betrayed the country that people the world over consider the epitome of freedom.

But soon after I met Mattie, at her house at the end of a mostly unpaved road in a wooded landscape in Virginia, I said that Libre was most meaningful not because of divorce or extortion, but for a more important reason. Whereas there are troops of lawyers employed to fight for one's freedom in matters of divorce or crimes against the government, there is only one Mattie Libre; and she fights for the bird held in the highest disrepute by the general public, the bird most maligned and misunderstood. That bird is the vulture; and Mattie believes in the freedom of vultures.

In the early days of a so far sunny and blue-skied spring, two weeks before Easter, I park my car in Mattie Libre's driveway, which runs alongside several animal enclosures. The vultures' cage is at the end of a dirt path, set back near the woods, beyond the meticulously constructed and clean pens for the other animals currently under Mattie's rehabilitative care: an assemblage of squirrels, several barred and screech owls, a red-tailed hawk, some seagulls, and several pigeons. Excited, Mattie leads me along the dirt path to introduce me to the injured black vultures and turkey vultures, birds whose digestive tracts contain acid strong enough to kill botulism and cholera. Once Mattie has restored the vultures to strength, they will fly off to serve again as proud members of America's cleanup crew, our waste removal workers of the wild, a job similar to the garbage collectors of the human world, that highly paid position because, who wants to do it?

I have come to Mattie Libre's place in the woods from my home near Washington, D.C., where, in the sky above the suburbs and the fringes of the city, black vultures and turkey vultures wheel and soar. They are the birds that, with a wingspan of five to six feet, several neighbors have mistakenly identified as eagles or hawks in flight. But unlike eagles and hawks, raptors that swoop down from the sky with outstretched talons to grab a fish or mouse out of its existence, vultures rarely do such things. In fact, whereas vultures historically have been included in the raptor family, there is now believed to be a genetic link between vultures and the stork family. Ancestry aside, turkey vultures and black vultures in America live a somewhat paradoxical, and to a certain extent precarious, existence: The rapid growth of the nation's roads and highways, on which millions of mammals are killed, provide vultures a steady source of food; but those same roads open the countryside to development. When a vulture lays only two eggs each season, most often on bare ground; when the chicks of those eggs are born closed-eyed and helpless, and require care from both parents; and when the birth and care and raising of the chicks necessitates an isolated area of scrubby, shrubby fields in which to parent, then a new housing development or office park in the vulture's landscape bulldozes the bird's chances to reproduce. I find it useful to remember how often

I take for granted the garbage collectors in my neighborhood, appreciating them only when, for some reason—a holiday, a snowstorm—they stop coming.

Mattie calls ahead to the vultures: "Hey everyone! What are you guys doing?" Standing before us are eight vulture rehabilitants dining on the heart, liver, and other assorted organs of a deer inside the twelve-by-twenty-eight-foot wood-and-wire cage, while twenty or more healthy, wild vultures gather at various places around the cage of those in recovery. Three of the wild black vultures drop from a tree and run along a path through the woods toward Mattie's voice. In body and movement, the birds resemble the velociraptors in Steven Spielberg's *Jurassic Park;* but unlike Spielberg's vicious hunters, the vultures are comical, playing and nipping at one another like dogs vying for a rolling ball. Six other vultures balance on their long legs and spindly feet, seemingly tiptoeing, in a somewhat balletic manner, around the ribcage and legs of the deer splayed across the wire mesh atop the cage. The remaining black and turkey vultures perch in the huge bare trees of the property or swoop down for a swipe at the meat and then swing back up.

"They hear my voice and come in," Mattie had said, somewhat shyly, yet proudly, when we began walking toward the birds. And I saw she was telling the truth. Circling overhead, vultures that likely had been uplifted for hours on the spiraling thermals of warm air above the earth, searching like novitiates for their idea of heaven—an animal's carcass—began descending when Mattie called. Attired in their black plumage, it was as though little nuns and priests of the wild, missionaries preaching the miracles of their regenerative powers to turn rotten flesh into food, were landing around us.

The eating of a carcass—it is what repulses us most about vultures, as we watch them plunge their bare heads into a body on the side of the road. But if an animal's service to humanity is a requirement for our considering them as necessary and important in our lives, then perhaps we must rethink the scene; and define more precisely the human and nonhuman characters roaming the altar of the earth. Imagine vultures as ministers, vultures sermonizing, for their human congregations, on the benefits of a purified landscape. Or ponder, even, the poetic nature of a turkey vulture, the way its Latin name, *Cathartes aura,* when loosely translated, transforms the bird metaphorically into a "cleansing breeze of light."

Mattie does not call in the healthy, wild birds for her own pleasure, though to be sure she enjoys their presence: "I love two things, children and animals. The most undesirable animals," she exclaims. "I don't know why. Pigeons, possums, vultures. I take them here." Vultures are social creatures, Mattie explains, which means they live in groups; and it is her hope that her rehabilitants, once they are released, will be allowed entrée into the vulture culture composed of the wild birds she calls in. Since there are only a handful of wildlife rehabilitators on the East Coast that accept vultures into their care, some of Mattie's patients were delivered from as far away as New Jersey or South Carolina, rejected by rehabbers in the birds' home states, where the birds' original social groups existed. Much like crows, vultures roost together at night. Black vultures roost in groups that, depending on number, may fill a few trees, whereas turkey vultures might mix with black vultures or roost in a small family group. Whoever sleeps together, it is thought that vultures—again like crows—share the day's news about food sources before they nod off. When morning arrives— and after the vultures' wings are soaked in the sun for warmth and vitamin D—the birds head out to work, with those who went hungry the day before following those who were more successful in locating where the latest death has occurred.

When I wonder about how a vulture discovers death, I remember that I always fail in my own searches for the remains or discarded body parts of animals—shed deer antlers, say, or an old skunk's skull in the woods.

Take a seat, then, if you will, on the wing of a turkey vulture that is in the sky searching for a dead animal below. From the bird's wing, you cannot see what the vulture sees, especially at this distance, which seems to be inching closer to the clouds. Nevertheless, you peek through the vulture's black fingers of feathers and see that on earth there are large tracts of green forest or beige fields, or specks of houses and roads and buildings, but not many specifics. To arrive high in the sky, the vulture has essentially opposed gravity by rising on an upward current of warm air called a thermal, which is heat rising off the earth. You are familiar with thermals and have seen them from a distance while driving, when, as the thermals rise a few feet into the air off a sizzling street, they look like water, like the earth's sweat dripping off its body. But a vulture is more intimate with the atmosphere; and it is said that, once in the air, vultures have the ability to see thermals dancing deep into the sky. When your vulture, at a lower altitude, flaps its wings, it is seeing and seeking another thermal. But now, because your vulture is floating like a kite and wobbling only occasionally, there is a steadiness in its flight, a long and repetitive circling that could lull you, if you were lying on its wing, into a sound sleep.

Sleeping, you might miss the fact that above your turkey vulture there are, soon enough, soaring black vultures, birds that with their diminished sense of smell rely primarily on sight eight times greater than yours to find a carcass below. Black vultures tag behind the equally excellent-sighted turkey vulture because the turkey's superior sense of smell lands everyone at the restaurant of death sooner rather than later. And so, with you asleep in its black satin sheets of feathers, the turkey vulture smells, from high in the air, through dense forest and canopy cover, a certain perfume of the earth, a cologne of blood and bones toward which it, you, and the black vultures begin to descend.

It was through what might be called the wildlife-rehabilitator grapevine of the greater Washington, D.C., metro area that I first heard about Mattie Libre. "She's got dozens of vultures," said one rehabber on the phone. "If you want vultures, get to Mattie . . . but . . . why, again, did you say you want vultures?"

A short answer to the question does not exist, though I knew, as

I tried to come up with something, that had I truly wanted to explain myself it would be necessary to admit to having fallen in love with an old, inquisitive, and skinheaded Andean condor I had met years before along a dusty, windswept road deep in the heart of Chilean Patagonia, at the tip of South America. This was where, before I'd roamed into the condor's life, I'd roamed through the lives of the more alluring animals in this edgy, daring, and virtually unpopulated landscape: guanacos dashing across the pampas, crested caracaras soaring over rolling hills, dolphins shooting out of the Strait of Magellan, sea lions lounging on glacier-edged inlets, and impervious penguins raising their babies in muddy dugouts amidst fifty-mile-an-hour winds. But of all these, it was the condor, the vulture, that stole my heart.

Not that this was the first time I'd seen an Andean condor. A few years prior to visiting Patagonia, when I was on a previous press trip in a remote Andean forest in the mountains of Ecuador, a condor just barely swept me under its massive wings as it was either flying toward or away from the group of us listening to our tour guide tout the richness of Ecuador's environment. It was an incident that served to remind the tour guide to express, somewhat bizarrely I thought, his pride in a South American ceremony performed with an Andean condor. As I remember his details, a condor is hung upside down from a branch or a piece of wood while men riding on horseback gallop by the bird, punching it repeatedly with their fists, until the bird dies.

A story with such vivid imagery tends to spur questions, such as, For what exactly is the ceremony? Though desperate attempts were made to understand the behavior in the context of the life of a poor, rural South American villager—which meant searching for some hint of religious significance to it all—nothing of substance turned up. Ceremony, it seemed, was simply euphemism for one's heinous participation in killing, viciously, brutally, and with total disregard for any notion of life, a defenseless vulture.

The mind, I think, tends to cache stories of such sadness deep inside the reference book of one's memory, lest they lead to a hovering and conscious sense of devastation for the world, which, in all honesty, they probably achieve in the end, anyway. Whereby ultimately they become useful for a subsequent experience, when at a turning point you are searching for a certain knowledge about how to proceed. And you know the answer is there, somewhere, on one or another of the dog-eared pages of your life, where passages have been highlighted and underlined, often repeatedly.

This is what happened on that dusty, windswept road in Patagonia, when, as I was traveling, and deadly thirsty, I noticed a nearly blown-over sign advertising that up ahead was not only Coca-Cola, but an Andean condor as well. Patagonia, in places, has that frontier-town feel of the American Old West, which means you never know if the weathered, distressed wooden buildings you come across every seventy or so miles are inhabited by the local gun-toting cowboy, or, in the case of the condor, the happy old grandfather with a big white smile and a herd of skinny grandchildren grinning at the American: me.

I noticed the condor as I passed it on the way to purchase my Coke from Grandpa, who seemed not to speak English. The bird was strutting around its pen, which was the shape of a rectangle, at least thirty feet long and twelve feet wide, fenced in by chicken wire, on which, at the gate, loosely hung a box with the word DONACIÓNES printed on it. An Andean condor is a big bird, weighing some thirty pounds and having a wingspan of ten to twelve feet. Keeping a condor means feeding a condor, which, being the type of animal it is, eats meat. The meat can be rotten meat the rest of us and most other creatures won't touch, but is, new or old, food one assumes is rather expensive for humans to acquire only to then give to a condor.

"*Mi amor, mi amor,*" the grandfather babbled, as he drank a cold beer and as I, sipping on my Coke, walked around the perimeter of the condor's cage, which was not at all covered, while the little granddaughters wove by me, running in their airy white dresses embroidered in colorful flowers.

The grandfather's *amor,* or love, seemed not to be one of the grandchildren swirling around me but rather the condor, the large, powerful bird that, if it could fly on its black and white wings, could soar to heights of fifteen thousand feet. The powerful yet captive bird that could, in a free life, be purifying the Patagonian landscape of disease-bearing carcasses; the bird that could be engaged in courting; or be laying its one egg, which the female does only every two years; or be raising the chick of that one egg, a responsibility that both condor parents participate in for just over two years. Instead, the large, powerful bird that stood beside me was, sadly, engaged in absolutely nothing that it could otherwise naturally be doing. And the longer I stood there, on this wind-cutting day when the sky was, by late afternoon, a deep tangerine, the more I noticed that the condor was fond of rubbing its wings against the wire of its enclosure.

"Why doesn't the condor fly away?" I asked the grandfather, hoping he might be able to speak a bit of English, and wondering why, without a top over the bird's cage, the condor didn't leave.

"*Mi amor. Mi chiquito.*"

"Your baby? *Su bebé chiquito?*" I asked in my broken and faulty Spanish. The condor was by this time following me with every change in direction I made, like a child playing tag, the outrageousness of which forced me to smile. When I stopped, the condor stopped and stood by me, scratching again against the wire.

"*Mi amor. Oooh. Sí. Sí. Shush, shhh,*" the grandfather said, slurping down the rest of his beer.

"*Dónde está condor?* Condor from . . . ?" I asked the man while the bird was now talking at me, even though condors, like all vultures, are technically voiceless. Lacking a syrinx, or vocal chords, vultures are said to only hiss and rattle, except when the male is courting a female and engages in verbal seduction of a *gock, gock* nature. But this vulture was making a *wuff* sound to me, something like a snorting puppy, while it stayed by my side.

"*Sí, uff, uff.*" The grandfather was watching carefully.

I started to think, then, of the Andean condor ceremony and asked, "Bird not *ceremonia* bird?" in my now pitiful English.

talks with vultures

"Ahhhaa, aha," the grandfather grinned, and sighed, *"Mi amor."*

It was futile. I reached my hand through a hole in the chicken wire to touch what I knew was not only a magnificent and increasingly rare creature, but now a tame vulture. The condor *wuffed* at me again, rubbed against my arm, and then partially opened its wings and began an awkward and tumbling sort of run toward, I imagined, the tangerine sky, only to come up short just as it crashed into the chicken wire. It then gathered in its wings and stumbled about. This was the condor's life now: the perpetually teasing sky; the hallucination of freedom.

"What does it eat?" I blurted out, angry and caught up in the maddening situation of the bird; angry and dreaming up some way to rescue the condor, momentarily forgetting that the grandfather did not speak English. There were no answers for this condor, trapped in its cage of loss and madness. Whatever the vulture had known before—in the pampas, the Andes, in its wild Patagonian places—it never would know again. The condor was caged by its own enormousness, tripping over its desires.

"Sí, mi amor, sí. . . shhh," the grandfather said, seemingly attempting to comfort the bird. "Yeah . . . yeah," the grandfather then said, turning toward me, "Ah, Buddy . . . *come pollo,* ah . . . chickens, eat lots-n-lots a chicken. *Donacióne?* Chicken *mucho dinero!"*

"Buddy?" I said, attempting to remain composed. "Never met a Buddy before," I said to the grandfather, but more so to the bird, as I rubbed his wings and began searching my reference book of memory, the dog-eared pages of the mind, where the highlighted passages, the knowledge one seeks, might pop out just now. Was it right to pay this man to keep an Andean condor captive? How much more or less evil than killing a condor outright was this bird's subdued life of subsidized torture? Would my donation be used to feed chicken to the vulture or beer to the man? Maybe the grandfather's sweet-talking to Buddy was all an act. Or not, perhaps he truly cherished the condor in the same way I had, in this short time, become attached to it. *Where is the page? Which underlined passage is the one?*

the hopes of snakes

. . .

Before leaving me by the vulture cage so that she can feed the baby squirrels sleeping inside the house, Mattie tells me about her mailman. About how fearful he is when he must deliver to her house boxes that, filled with mealworms, are marked "live animals." About how the mailman hurries to her porch, hunched over the box, hiding his face for fear the vultures know he's carrying food and will swoop down to steal the box, perhaps picking at the mailman's tender skin and lithe muscles in the process. It seems not to have made an impression on the mailman that Mattie has told him repeatedly, in her effort to calm and comfort him, that the mealworms are for the small songbirds she rehabilitates. "But every time," she says, laughing, "he hunches over that box!"

I think of the mailman while I watch the several wild birds and the rehabilitants tearing at the deer's tawny-colored fur and bloody body with their hooked beaks. Beaks made for the hard work of ripping through the tapestry of bones, organs, and muscles that once, when the body parts were stitched together, formed the beautiful deer that ran in front of the car that hit it, which is how it ended up here, donated to Mattie from the wildlife officials of her local government. I notice, as I stand fairly close listening to the vultures grunt and lightly argue like dogs over who gets what to eat, that, similar to the mailman, I have my own unease. The unease of hearing the unsettling sound of the deer's ligaments ripping, the unease of smelling the overwhelming cloud of blood that seems to hang in the air. Flies force their way around the vultures, as though buzzing with joy over the meal; still, none of it is especially easy to witness. Though perhaps this is one point: that the workings of the world, so wondrously evolved, are not necessarily meant to be easily taken in and understood. Some relationships in the nonhuman world may be less like the ease of a catchy Broadway tune and more like the complicated disharmonies of Miles Davis or Philip Glass; but, either way, we are witnesses and participants in the artistry of evolution.

One day in the future, when Mattie's vultures are healthy

talks with vultures

enough to fly away—the one that was shot with an arrow, the other that was hit by a car and left on the side of the road, a third that arrived with a massive infection on its head—any of their lives would be a life that Buddy, the Andean condor, would have deserved. I watch the vultures dine on the deer meat that is not terribly unlike someone eating steak tartare or sushi. I smell the deer blood clouded in my nose and mouth; and its scent differs little from that known by any woman who, during the birth of her children, spilled carafes of her own red magic into the world. And I think of Buddy, and of the money I gave to the grandfather out of sympathy for a vulture that, sadly and forever, would be tame and easy to watch.

I leave the vultures eating and go to find Mattie inside her house, where I can gape at the tiny infant squirrels sucking down a formula of squirrel milk into their sweet, silver bodies. In Mattie's living area, which is separate from the indoor rehabilitation facility, photos of her grandchildren and photos, drawings, and paintings of an assortment of animals—a crow, a raccoon, a possum, and a vulture, among others—splatter the walls. Mattie calls me to the back porch and pulls out an envelope brimming with photos of Clem, a black vulture that, when he was six months old, was delivered in perfect condition to Mattie. Perfect except in one way, which was somewhat similar to the way of Buddy: Clem had imprinted on humans when an infant, which meant Clem would come to understand Mattie as a mother of sorts or, more technically defined, as his "object of habitual trust." With hard work, one can reverse a tame animal's association to humans; but turning an imprinted animal back to a wild animal is a formidable undertaking, and nearly impossible. Nevertheless, Mattie Libre saw no other choice than to cleanse Clem of his humanness. "It was," she explains, "the only way he could be free."

Training Clem in the manners of a true vulture took four years. So young and attached to humans on his arrival, he spent his first year growing up and forming a skeleton of independence. The next year, Mattie released him not far from the house, secure in her belief that he would come back if necessary. Which he did, "every day that year," she remembers. That also was when he brought home another vulture, and they became the duo Mattie called Clem & Company. She riffles through the photos to show me one of Clem perched on the riding mower while Mattie cuts the lawn, explaining that Company is in the woods, some distance away, waiting for Clem to cut loose. The next year, the third, Clem dropped by twice a month the entire year. He stuck by Mattie's side on those visits, following her around the yard. He waited outside the kitchen window for her to finish her morning coffee. He played, as does a chimpanzee, with his reflection in a mirror Mattie set up in the yard. He tugged on shoes and on "anything yellow," Mattie remembers. "He loved anything yellow."

Then came spring and the changing light in the sky, when Clem flew off with Company.

A year passed.

Until "last Easter," Mattie says. "He came back on Easter Day, but I haven't seen him since."

Mattie is a practical, wise, and caring woman; and she cautions me against making any mystical or spiritual connections between herself and what she does for these animals. "This is what I do. It is simple," she says. "Someone else works at a bank. I do this. I am not special." Still, I cannot help but file away the irony of a vulture, the so-called bird of death, reappearing on what is for Christians one of the most important and festive days of the year, the day of the Resurrection of Christ.

Though perhaps something less about the festivities of the human world and more about the revival of the wild world had triggered the return of Clem—who after a year away was by then a vulture fully attuned to the sky, a vulture sensitive to rising thermals, to wind, sunshine, rain, and night. Perhaps Clem was called by the season, by the ancient way it slowly massages forth life, something he felt as a blossoming of energy shivering through his feathers, the same energy mammals might feel in their fur, reptiles in their skin, and trees in their buds. On the Easter Day Clem re-

talks with vultures

turned, the sky—in its pink and orange light, in its air currents and temperatures—was much like a day the previous spring. And so perhaps at that point Clem flew back into the winds of his memories, where, like a petal trembling in his consciousness, there was something that made his life as a free vulture possible. If Clem's had been a human life, his freedom would've been his turning point, the most dog-eared page, the most underlined passage of his story. And so though his return coincided with Easter, for the free bird that Clem had now become, it was more that the northern spring equinox had occurred and that, soon after, a full moon had lit the sky, and that somewhere, in all the beauty he had come to know, was a flowering image of Mattie Libre.

Mattie speaks now of Clem in the way a parent speaks of their grown children, as if all the difficult, exceedingly complicated, yet lovely eighteen years flew by in just a precious few seasons of celebrations, holidays, graduations, vacations, fun. And as she talks of vultures, of Clem, she looks toward the sky. Easter is almost here.

Acknowledgments

I am grateful to many whose wisdom, enthusiasm, and kindness steered me along the paths I needed to go.

At times, a writer needs a host—an editor and mentor—to feed her hunger, to be, now and then, the center and blood of the writer's world. Though privately I have in essence said something similar to the editor and writer John A. Murray, I wish to thank him now, publicly, for his generous spirit, his guidance, for the wise host he has been to me for many years.

It is true that Steve Hutkins, my graduate adviser at New York University, freed me into the fields of New York City: fields of questions, curiosity, and feeling. He opened the gates.

Several people have turned a chapter for me here and there: writer, editor, and University of Houston professor Terrell Dixon kept me like a spider in his web, encouraging me to spin my particular silk; the supportive words of poet Pattiann Rogers were invaluable; novelist Brian Morton gave, early on, his considered thoughts; and the former yet longtime editor of *Potomac Review,* Eli Flam, took me under his Washington, D.C., literary wing.

A book that concerns nonhuman animals is difficult to write without help from the biologists, naturalists, and wildlife rehabilitators—and all the associated creatures—who gave me the great privilege of entering their worlds: Chris Nadareski and the peregrine falcons of New York City; Robert Cook and the black racers of Floyd Bennett Field in Brooklyn; Rob Gibbs and the coyotes of Montgomery County, Maryland; Diana Yates and the long-legged wading birds of the Arthur Kill; Mattie Libre and the vultures of the Washington metro area; Melanie Marshall and Edgar Allen Crow of Meadowside Nature Center in Rockville, Maryland; and

Chris Montuori and Polly Hoffmann—and the geese and hundreds of squirrels, birds, and other rehabilitants—of Second Chance Wildlife Center in Gaithersburg, Maryland.

For the long walks—through the hot and cold city, along sooty urban rivers and salty shorelines, around butterfly ponds, in damp woods—I wish to thank Kirk Mettam, who has accompanied me since childhood, really; Will Nixon and Emma Segal, always curious and willing; Marisa Matero and Kevin Maury, deep-spirited, both; and Nancy Gagliardi and Declan Denehan, the New Yorkers.

I am deeply grateful for my past five years with the Brookmont Arts Alliance, in which the writers Jean Johnson, Adrienne Hand, Peter Ainslie, Kate Robinson, Rebecca Petillo, and the artists Raye Leith and Janet Wittenberg are my kindred spirits.

I would have little time for writing without help from the wonderful women who love and care for my children as their own: Patricia Couturier, Maria Perez, Jean Mettam, Catherine Young, and Jeannette Ralda. I wish also to thank sweet Joseph Pritchard and my friend Sharon Pritchard.

Much gratitude to Luis Laso, Lisa Clarke, and Eric Couturier for their helping hands.

I am blessed to move within the circles of certain individuals who in their own ways illuminate for me the complex connections between the human, the nonhuman, and the soul: Hallie S. Lovett, Ph.D., Gail Couturier, Kate White, Rosemary Dickerson, Grace Ogden, Barbara Tufty, Julie Seiler, and Kenneth Ingham.

My literary agent, Stephanie von Hirschberg, has seen me through the evolution and has offered not only her guidance and counsel, but also, to the world, to animals, and to me, the gift of her heart. Thank you.

For her faith in what was to come and for what is here, for her intuitiveness and vision, I give Joanne Wyckoff, my editor at Beacon Press, deepest thanks.

One's family of origin plants seeds. In ways difficult to express, I am grateful to my mother, Patricia Ann Candlish Couturier, for what she taught me about the music of a mind; to my father,

158

Adolphe Pierre Couturier, for, long ago, all the wild ones he placed in my hands; to my brother, Steven Couturier, for teaching me patience; and to my sister, Lynn Couturier-Verheugen, for her endless good-naturedness.

Of course without Kirk Mettam and our lovely daughters, Madeleine and Lucienne, a certain river would run dry, the bird would perch flightless, the green life would diminish. Thank you for your company on this great expedition.

Finally, a few words of gratitude for autumn and winter in the mid-Atlantic, for the trance in which the seasons place me, for the way the earth smells then and its clear air. Most of all, though, the animals—those at the edges and those in my arms, those who hide yet watch, hope, and know. Thank you for your stories, for the occasions to sit close.